Compiled and edited by The MaxKol Institute

Published by The Maxkol Institute © Copyright 1998

ISBN: 0-9668056-2-3

Published in the United States of America

Copies of this book may be obtained by contacting:
The Maxkol Institute, 1301 Moran Rd., Suite 303
Sterling, VA 20166
Tel: (703) 421-1300
Fax: (703) 421-1133
E-Mail: maxkol@msn.com
Websites: www.maxkol.org

D07331169

Declarations

Since the abolition of Canon 1399 and 2318 of the former Canonical Code, publications about new appearances, revelations, prophecies, miracles, etc., have been allowed to be distributed and ready by the faithful without the express permission of the Church, providing they contain nothing which contravenes faith and morals. This means no imprimatur is necessary when distributing information on new apparitions not yet judged by the Church. The authors wish to manifest unconditional submission to the final and official judgement of the Magisterium of the Church regarding any events presently under investigation.

In Lumen Gentium, Vatican II, Chapter 12, the Council Fathers urged the faithful to be open and attentive to the ways in which the Holy Spirit continues to guide the Church, including private revelations. We hear: "Such gifts of grace, whether they are of special enlightenment or whether they are spread more simply and generally, must be accepted with gratefulness and consolation, as they are specially suited to and useful for, the needs of the Church. Judgements as to their genuineness and their correct use lies with those who lead the Church and those whose special task is not to extinguish the Spirit but to examine everything and keep that which is good.

The title and cover of this book was chosen by our heavenly mother.

She gave the following explanation: "It represents the Sacred Heart of Our Lord and Savior Jesus Christ and the Immaculate Heart of your heavenly mother. Through my Immaculate Heart, with my beloved spouse, the Holy Spirit, will the gates open into The New Era of Peace and a New Heaven. From which **both hearts** will **triumph**, in victory over the evil one, one in union with each other, as I am one in union with our Lord and Savior Jesus Christ. Through our Creator, all things are made possible. We do all for the Honor and Glory, for Our Father in Heaven.

Glory Be to the Father,
And to the Son,
And to the Holy Spirit.
As it was in the beginning,
Is now and ever shall be,
World without end. Amen

Our Father, Who art in heaven
Hallowed be Thy name.
Thy Kingdom come, Thy Will be done
On earth, as it is in heaven.
Give us this day our daily bread,
And forgive us our trespasses
As we forgive those who trespass against us.
And lead us not into temptation,
And deliver us from evil. Amen

Hail Mary, full of grace
The Lord is with thee.
Blessed art thou among women,
And blessed is the fruit of thy womb, Jesus.
Holy Mary, Mother of God,
Pray for us sinners,
Now, and at the hour of our death. Amen.

My Father's House
Retreat Center
39 North Moodus Road
PO Box 22
Moodus, CT 06469

Tel 860-873-1581
Fax 860-873-2357

Co-Directors
Fr. William McCarthy, MSA
Sr. Bernadette Sheldon, CSJ

September 10, 1998

We are writing to give our discernment and also support to the ministry of Joseph Della Puca and Denise Curtin, who are from Connecticut. We have known Joseph and Denise for about three years and have watched them grow closer and closer to Our Lord and Our Blessed Mother. Both are sincere, deeply prayerful and open to the Spirit. They pray and minister together with the full blessing of Joseph's father and Denise's husband and family.

We have visited the prayer room where they primarily pray for hours at a time and claim to receive visitations and apparitions from Mary and Jesus. Judging from the fruit of their lives and the content of their messages, we discern them to be authentic. Joseph and Denise are humble in the manner they present the messages received from Mary. The messages are both personal and more global.

We recommend your support of both these visionaries and their messages.

Yours in Christ,

Fr. Bill McCarthy, MSA   Sr. Bernadette Sheldon, CSJ

Two Hearts As One

TABLE OF CONTENTS

DEDICATION

To Our Heavenly Father, our Creator, for it is through Him that all things are made possible.

To Our Lord and Savior, Jesus Christ, Whose infinite Love for mankind is like that of a rainbow, it has no beginning and no end.

To the Holy Spirit, Who gives us the enlightenment and discernment so we may receive, understand and speak the Word of God.

To our heavenly mother, for all of her teachings, and for leading us to Our Lord and Savior, Jesus Christ.

ACKNOWLEDGEMENT

We want to thank our Heavenly Father for the Divine Invitation which allowed us to become vessels of the Word of God.

Our families have become an invaluable source of support for both of us: Denise's husband, Frank, and their daughters Chanel and Krystle; her sister Deborah; Sisto, Joseph's father; and sisters Linda, MaryAnn and Shirley. No matter how difficult and insurmountable the problems were, their loyalty, faith, trust and prayers have carried us through these difficult periods.

We are thankful for the assistance of our Spiritual Director, Father Bill McCarthy, from My Father's House in Moodus, Connecticut, for his guidance and discernment for us on our spiritual journey. No matter what hour we called he was there for us, with confident wisdom, guidance and discernment on our spiritual journey. We are also thankful to Sister Bernadette of My Father's House for her tireless help.

We are indebted to Josyp Terelya, through the guidance of our heavenly mother, for offering his spiritual support and providing the artwork for this publication. Josyp has spent many hours through the power of the Holy Spirit creating these beautiful pictures to enhance our heavenly mother's messages.

We also wish to thank Joe Hunt, Dr. Joseph Vitolo, Aleisha Beaulieu, Deborah Albaitis, all of whom have spent many hours indexing, proofreading and other miscellaneous tasks preparing this manuscript for its publication.

Finally, we would like to thank Ted Flynn, President of the Maxkol Institute, author of The Thunder of Justice and the producer of the films *Prophecy and the New Times*, and *The Key To The Triumph – The Final Marian Dogma, Coredemptrix, Mediatrix, and Advocate.* Also, many thanks to Maria Van der Hoof of the MaxKol Institute.

And this is life eternal, that they
might know thee the only true God, and
Jesus Christ, whom thou hast sent.

I have glorified thee on the earth: I
have finished the work which thou gavest me to do.
(John 17:3-4)

Joseph and Denise

JOSEPH DELLAPUCA

Joseph DellaPuca was born in 1956 and is an executive living in Southington, Connecticut. He is a devoted Catholic and attends Immaculate Conception Catholic Church, in Southington, CT.

Joseph's first mystical experience began during 1993, in Meriden, Connecticut, where he heard a rumor that the Blessed Virgin Mary was appearing locally. Skeptical at first, his father and sister went to the apparition site on a bitter cold night in January of that year.

The next morning, when Joseph questioned his father about the alleged appearance of the Mother of God, his father said that approximately 200 people were there praying the most holy Rosary. In the middle of winter there was a Rose of Sharon bush in full bloom where the Blessed Mother was appearing, and it was January in New England. After hearing this, Joseph decided to visit the apparition site.

While visiting the site and praying the Rosary with a group of people, Joseph noticed a bright light appearing in front of the Rose of Sharon bush. Within that light appeared the most beautiful woman he had ever seen, dressed in white and holding crystalline Rosary beads in her hands. He fell to his knees and continued to pray the Rosary, while informing his sister, who was praying alongside him, that the Blessed Virgin Mary was standing in front of the Rose of Sharon bush dressed in white. From that moment, Joseph's life was changed as he heard the Mother of God ask him to change his way of life and to make our Lord and Savior, Jesus Christ his first priority.

Before Our Lady contacted Joseph, he had not been versed in praying the Rosary, nor could he immediately name all the

Mysteries of the Rosary. He had previously gone to Mass, but mostly out of obligation.

Without questioning the Blessed Mother, Joseph quickly agreed to what she asked. Subsequently, he felt himself drawn with a fervor to Scripture, praying daily the fifteen-decade Rosary, attending Mass every day, and for the first time in twelve years, went to Confession.

Joseph found himself strongly attracted to collect religious objects, and transformed his bedroom into a special spiritual atmosphere that helped him focus on meditation, prayer, and peace. This helped him change his once materialistic life to a far more spiritual one. Gone were the worry, stress, and the constant striving for success, as defined by our culture. All was replaced by his new dedication to God, and he filled his non-working hours with prayer and active involvement in prayer meetings.

In the Spring of 1995, Joseph started to notice a light fragrance of roses coming from the Our Lady of Fatima statue in his room while he was praying. This rose fragrance became progressively stronger each day, and at times, could be detected throughout his whole neighborhood. Often, neighbors would comment on this beautiful fragrance, wondering where it came from, as there were no rose bushes anywhere in the vicinity.

During the Autumn of 1995, after a night of prayer, Joseph awakened in the morning to a very faint fragrance of roses while in bed. To his amazement, the fragrance was emanating from his own body. Our heavenly mother had graced him with the *gift of roses*, which would become stronger, especially after prayer. This fragrance has been noticed and commented upon by many people who come into contact with him. This special gift continues to remain with Joseph today, and becomes prominent at unexpected times.

One evening while in prayer, Joseph noticed a bright light in his room, emanating from above the Rosa Mystica statue of the Blessed Mother. Within this light appeared the Blessed Mother, who said to Joseph, "Do not be frightened, my son, for I am your heavenly mother. You have found favor with God, our Father in Heaven. I, your heavenly mother, have come to teach you the ways of Our Heavenly Father."

During all subsequent apparitions Joseph has been graced to see, hear and converse with the Mother of God. She would appear two or three times every week during his prayers, teaching Joseph the meaning of the Mysteries of the Rosary, Scripture, and also a detailed three-level preparation for prayer. These teachings caused Joseph to become totally transformed spiritually and emotionally, bringing him into a closer personal relationship with God and all those in Heaven.

In the beginning, the apparitions were a few minutes in duration, but became progressively longer each week. Each day became a stepping stone, developing Joseph gradually into a state of unconditional love for our Lord. This process was to assist him to refine his soul and to make it a more pure receptacle to receive the Word of God.

For the first several months, the Blessed Mother taught Joseph to feel the Divine Love that our Lord constantly pours forth, and to share that Love with others through acts of forgiveness. He was taught that we are not to judge, but to love one another as our Lord loves us. He learned that it is only through prayer that one will be able to attain the love of truth, for truth is the Word of God. Our heavenly mother has asked that we pray unceasingly, and to follow the holy path of God through fasting, penance, and bearing His fruit through our good works.

Joseph has a B.S. in Biology and Masters Degree in Immunopharmacology from the University of Connecticut. He also has a Masters Degree in Hospital Administration and Public Health from Yale University. He has worked in Hospital Administration and is presently working in Long Term Care.

DENISE CURTIN

Denise Curtin, an identical twin, is from a family of six children, and is employed as an executive assistant at a health care facility. She is married, the mother of two children, and has lived in Manchester, Connecticut for 23 years. Mrs. Curtin is a devout Catholic and attends daily Mass at Assumption Catholic Church in Manchester, Connecticut.

Denise met Joseph DellaPuca, who was one of her co-workers, in the Summer of 1995. The following Spring she had a strong attraction to the presence of Our Lord during Mass and when she prayed the Stations of the Cross. It was then that she discovered the strong Love our Lord has for us, and how much He yearns for our love in return. Several months later, Denise and her family became actively involved in a weekly Marian Cenacle.

While praying in the Cenacle she noticed the light fragrance of roses around her and felt a breeze caressing her face. It was there that she became aware that the Mother of Jesus Christ was asking her to change her way of life and to make Our Lord her first priority. Soon after, Denise's life was committed to a total unconditional love for Christ through the Blessed Mother. She would attend several prayer Cenacles per week, and pray the fifteen decades of the Rosary each day. She noticed that her spiritual appreciation of the Mass was steadily increasing. In the Fall of 1996, at the Consecration of the Mass, her heart began to beat very rapidly and a very warm presence consumed her body. This phenomenon not only continues to happen to this day whenever she attends Mass, but also during the reading of the Gospel.

While sitting at her desk at work one afternoon, Denise was struck by a powerful fragrance of roses emanating from

Joseph DellaPuca's office. She felt a strong sense of peace and love. He explained that the Blessed Mother had been present for a few minutes and gave him a message. Whenever Joseph and Denise were present in meetings at work, frequently a strong fragrance of roses would fill the room.

Over the next several months, Denise gradually underwent a spiritual transformation that changed the direction of her life, committing her heart and soul to the care of the requirements of heaven. While attending her first Healing Mass at a local church, she became "slain in the Holy Spirit." She describes this phenomena as "...being showered with brilliant rays of light, with a very rapid beating of the heart and a very warm sensation throughout the body."

Denise describes our heavenly mother as appearing around the age of fifteen, thin and about 5 feet, 2 inches in height. She has chestnut hair, parted in the middle and wavy, and extending below her shoulders. Her face is porcelain white and thin, with brown eyes. A majority of the time she appears with a powder blue veil that extends down past her waist. She wears a white dress, which exposes her neck to the collarbone, with a gold rope around her waist. She appears with her hands together in prayer with her Rosary beads, which are either golden or crystalline. She appears in three dimensional spirit form, enveloped in a very bright, blue/white light throughout the entire apparition.

In the Fall of 1997, Denise began having mystical experiences with Our Lord through inner locutions, after receiving the Holy Eucharist during Mass. (Inner locution means hearing a divine voice internally, while no one else near the individual can hear it). The inner locutions are short in duration.

Several times, Denise has experienced the majestic display of the *miracle of the sun*, similar to that witnessed by many thousands of people at Fatima, Medjugorje, and other apparition sites. She sees the sun pulsating very rapidly, dropping down from the sky, and going back up to its original position. There then appears a brilliant colored rainbow around the sun, encircled by what appears to be a host similar to the consecrated Host at Mass.

Our Heavenly mother has taught Denise and Joseph not only the three levels of prayer preparation, but to spiritually prepare souls to attain the greatest communion with God to properly receive His Divine Love. While in prayer, they have experienced their souls being lifted from their bodies and transported to view Heaven. They describe Heaven as brilliant colors unlike any of those on Earth, with a very intense feeling of Love and Peace. During this spiritual state of vision, they met our Lord and Savior for the first time. They describe Him dressed in a white gown, with brown hair parted in the middle, extending to His shoulders, with dark brown eyes. He told them that they would spread the Word of God, and that it would start out slowly and increase with time. They were to gather the sheep and bring them to the Shepherd.

On the 13th of each month, and on other unannounced days, our heavenly mother appears to Denise and Joseph with a message that is to be given to the world. She begins her evening with a personal message intended for them, then leads them in the most holy Rosary. Upon completion, they have an open conversation with our heavenly mother that is often very personal, like a mother with her children. Besides giving them a worldwide message for all of her children, she teaches them the words, ways and means of God through examples. Our heavenly mother has given them numerous prayers and fourteen special prayers which they recite each night, per her request.

Denise is an Executive Assistant in a Long Term Healthcare facility. She is married to Frank Curtin and has two children, Chanel and Krystle.

Coredemptrix, Mediatrix, and Advocate

Coredemptrix, Mediatrix, and Advocate

If history has shown us a single thing it is that mankind continues to make the same mistakes. The often used phrase 'history repeats itself' is a true one. It is true, because man hasn't changed much from the time he was made. There is Original Sin and it has been with us for a long time. The lower nature is in combat with the higher nature on a never-ending basis. We may argue, but we see the reality of this around us no matter where we look. Satan rejected the things of God and has been seeking targets ever since. Although battles are all on different levels, they are all tiny in comparison to the war for the soul of man.

There are physical truths and scientific truths. Who can doubt that the law of gravity is a physical truth? It would be a very foolish person who would climb to the top of a tall building and argue with this physical truth. History, fact, and precedent show it to be inevitably true. You may argue all day, but you will loose. Science, chemistry, physics, and natural law have similar examples of truth which apply. They may be disputed, but in the end the laws of nature are fixed and will follow the course of which they were intended. Bacteria in a wound will cause infection. A prick to the finger will draw blood. An arrow shot into the air will descend. A moving machine is best lubricated by an oil rather than molasses. The list is endless for the examples of physical and natural law in our midst each waking hour.

Spiritual laws are fixed and they may not be manipulated or coerced in any way. Illusion is not an option. They may be bent and concealed for a period of time but the truth will always be found out. Time will produce truth. All physical and natural law is subordinate to them, not the other way around. The embodiment of truth is in the person of Jesus

Christ. We are living a mystery that is best just appreciated rather than analyzed and bisected. And when we surrender our will to these eternal truths, the machinery runs better and there is more harmony in the process.

There has been a truth where wars have been fought, territories won and lost, crowns surrendered, and lineage shattered. The lower nature of man has not said 'yes' as a lowly handmaid once did nearly two thousand years ago because 'yes' can only be said in a spiritually elevated state. Where all occupants of the family were born on the wrong side of the tracks, a countersign of all countersigns was born to inject a new life into the world. As the scribe said, "Can anything good come from Nazareth?" The things of the flesh can only be understood by the flesh and the things of the spirit can only be understood by the spirit. It takes a person of wisdom to understand wisdom. History shows us the things of the Spirit will not be generally understood, and may not be accepted. It was the High Priest who denied the invitation and was struck dumb but Mary said 'yes.'

Our intellectual pride and cultural bias all point us away from this mystery. For if we adhere to and defend it, we are automatically dismissed as an intellectual pygmy. We do not have the right pedigree, we lack spiritual development, scholastically we lack sophistication, and if we knew better we would not even open our mouth on the subject. It is not the passport to higher incomes, academic advancement, promotions in the workplace, conversations on the first tee, and it is best not brought up in mixed company for it is certainly the quickest way to clear the room or put a damper at the dining room table. And because we have denied divinity in our age, we have carnal, banal, inane, callous, and cynical vulgarity in our culture. This is our fruit.

She is the Blessed Mother, Queen of Heaven and Earth and the Mother of Jesus Christ, God in the flesh. Her titles are too numerous to mention and they are only matched by her controversy and mystery. Throughout history, armies have marched to what she has asked. For those unwilling or unable to dialogue on her role in Scripture or Sacred Tradition, they put her as the fourth member of the Trinity as a way to dodge the issue of who she really is. It's the easy way out and will not tax any cerebral tissue. No spiritual sweat is expended. A pithy saying or witticism can dismiss who she is and what is her role. False cultural inheritance seeps through the cracks to pollute the pile of what is good and true. The philosophy of heaven's detractors has won no victories. The atheist leaves no useful or good legacy for humanity. There are responses born of the flesh and of the Spirit. The friends of the Lord have never been the majority in any civilization.

However, what is born of the flesh will be of the flesh, and what is of God will be God. History has again been a good teacher. But maybe because media and video have made us more illiterate than the previous generations to the great classical teachings, we fail to see the eternal truths that previous generations understood at least a little bit better. Maybe it's because we are Westerners and more specifically Americans that we fail to see the truth. Science and technology are the new gods of our age. Each age has one, as each age has an 'ism' to worship because of its bankrupt soul. Each age needs to invent one so it can pour forth its energy into some sort of philosophy. It fills the vacuum. There is no requirement to think. There is no requirement to confront ourselves. For if we did we would need to change. But Scripture is the barometer of truth. It is an immovable feast and the rules will not bend for anyone. It shows us many irrefutable truths and something we see time and again is that the Lord works through the few because it is the few who say 'yes.'

This thinking can easily breed a bunker mentality which can make one feel they hold the truths to the Kingdom of Heaven. If not my way, no way. But, Scripture shows us on nearly every page that Heaven's ways are not our ways. Yahweh calls out Abraham on a singular basis and gives him a job to do. He did the same with Noah, Moses, Lot and his family, Gideon, Daniel, Isaiah and for all others that said 'yes' to what was asked. Oftentimes under duress, the unknown, as well as difficult and humiliating circumstances. What would we think if we were asked to sacrifice our son on an altar? Build an ark and be the laughing stock of friends and neighbors? Stand before a Pharaoh with a 400 year history of free labor so your kingdom could live in ease and comfort. We forget that these people were human with natures like ours and judging by the common response, they found it difficult. Jonah hiding under the shade of the tree in humiliation for what he had prophesied had not come true. The prophecy never materializes because the people did put on sackcloth and ashes in repentance as was asked. Elijah saying he was the only righteous man and moaning to God about his fidelity and thinking no one else had the agenda of the Lord in mind. Yahweh said otherwise. Job thought he had figured out the mystery of the universe until Yahweh spoke from the tempest in the 38th chapter asking him if he knew the secrets of the universe. Meekness and humility had suddenly returned.

Why some people respond to the request of Heaven is not always known. There seems to be no respect for title or occupation and how much is grace versus our saying 'yes' is not always a clear issue. There is clearly a 'ten talent' and a 'one talent' person. Jesus spoke to Peter on how he could be sifted like wheat if it were not for the grace that was given to

him. There are clearly those who do seem to be specially
favored from a human standpoint, for with the bouquet of
roses will come thorns. No one totally escapes.

In the annals of time no other individual seems to illustrate
this more than our heavenly mother. She speaks only seven
times in Scripture and every single word or action has been
analyzed by scholars and theologians to give interpretation to
it. Her words are rooted in logic and mystery. She was from
the very beginning God's best. A vessel needed to be
created without spot or blemish to house God Himself. It
needed to be by design a perfect vessel with no stain. He is
God and our lack of knowledge about the secrets of the
universe, we must accept what God the Father in unity with
the Trinity chose to do. Here lies the taproot of why some
understand and others do not. To even begin to grasp the
meaning of life we must decide to put ourselves on the plain
of how God sees things and then we must adapt to that
structure and design. To do it any other way is a painful way
paved with undue hardship, difficulty and pain. Every writer
at some time wants to write their best; every builder at some
time wants to build their best; every sculptor at some time
wants to sculpt a Pieta; every painter at some time would like
to have a masterpiece to his name; and the Blessed Mother is
God's best. She was perfect because this is the way God
wanted her to be. She is the short way to the Heart of the
Father.

From the announcement of the angel calling Mary 'blessed'
among woman, and all generations would call her blessed,
she said 'yes.' Startled at first for sure, but the answer was
still 'yes.' How often our answer is 'no' as we fail to open
the chambers of our heart to the 'yes.' Where Eve had said
'no' to the graces given her, Mary had become the new Eve.
She knew the role that she was to have as well as that of her
Son. Can you imagine for a single second if we knew that

this was the destiny of your only child and then endure it? When it was finally time for the cross, on not one occasion did she try to talk Him from the cup that He knew that He must drink from. Even his good friend Simon Peter talked to Him in the spirit of the flesh and Jesus said, "get behind me Satan," for Jesus knew where this thought was from. Her privileges, grace, will, and strength were unique gifts.

Her final words to the world in Scripture were, "Do whatever He tells you," as they were uttered at the wedding feast of Cana. She was never concerned about her agenda, but His, always in the back round doing the will of the Father. While all His friends, apostles, disciples scattered out of fear, she knelt and wept at the foot of the cross suffering mystically the wounds of His passion. Even one of His good friends said on three separate occasions, "I don't know the man." Watching at the foot of the cross the humiliation the Son of Man must endure to redeem the world of enslavement from sin. It is not hard for us to imagine, it is virtually impossible. Only at times do we understand the breadth and the width of what was accomplished. When we do get a glimpse of the profound mystery we are usually in the presence of a Monstrance or a Tabernacle.

All of what Jesus said was not understood. When He said to the rulers of Judea, "tear down this temple and in three days I will build it back again," He was saying something that was going to be based in the future. The response was, "how can this be when this temple took over fifty years to build." There was not even a remote understanding what Jesus was talking about by those around Him. His close friends were dumbfounded. Prophecy has a veil over it with an allegorical and metaphorical meaning to what is being said. Such is the case with so many visionaries today. They do not know precisely what they are saying other than they have been asked to say it. They are pots of clay being asked to be a voice for the things of God just as Moses and others were asked.

There are several camps following apparitions today: those who believe in anything and those who believe in nothing. There are those who believe only when the Church approves the apparition and it works its way into Magisterial thinking over time, and there are those who believe what is only in Scripture (Sola Scriptura) which will never bring a person down the wrong path, but on the other hand, they do not remain open to the Holy Spirit, missing some of the banquet feast. And lastly, those who are openly hostile to what the Holy Spirit is doing in our midst.

The vast majority of the population is in a state of denial about the spiritual nature of what is going on around us. Hence only few in number responding to the requests of Heaven in the biblical examples cited above. Logic, prudence, wisdom, circumstance, social, political, financial, and the entire realm of spiritual and physical evidence point to the fact mankind is in deep trouble. Those observing with spiritual eyes see the signs as others remain impervious to them, taking another page out of history. So Heaven in its great mercy has sent its most precious vessel to be the prophetess of our age to warn and guide man in these difficult shoals. It is a supreme act of grace and mercy from Heaven to send the mother of Jesus as that person. The times must warrant such a person who has such influence of grace.

The signs around us are staggering: weeping statues, rosary beads turning gold, mystical phenomena, nearly one thousand pages of Father Stefano Gobbi speaking to the Order of Melchizedek, the Levites, the priests, with the December 31, 1997 and last message titled, "All Has Been Revealed To You." Over twenty five years of messages given to those wishing to listen about where mankind has been, where it is, and where it is headed. They are unprecedented in all of history in such detail. What does Heaven know we do not? The gift of Medjugorje happening since 1981, is a veritable fountain of grace, love, and healing to those who wish to drink from the cup. John Paul II, who is immolated on the altar of suffering as he bears witness to the truth is the gift for our times. The prophecy of Don Bosco concerning the Twin Pillars of the Church, the Eucharist and the Blessed Mother is predicted to take place before the end of this century. Fatima, Akita, Rue du Bac, Guadalupe, Amsterdam and others amount to an act of love, warnings guiding the footsteps of humanity.

In no way are the messages given to us by Heaven throughout history philosophical or political. They are messages of love as a mother to her child wanting the best for that child even if it is a bit painful. The most controversial issue during the day of Jesus was Roman occupation, which meant taxes for the Jews. All other issues to the Jews were insignificant in comparison to this issue. Yet, Jesus never addressed this issue until asked, and even then, He gave a one sentence response. "Give to Caesar the things of Caesar and to God the things of God." It infuriated the law givers because Jesus couldn't be manipulated. Heaven is most interested in things of the heart, because when this is in proper order, everything else falls neatly into place. This is why the primary cry at all of the apparition sites is that of conversion. Then there are things which should follow; a new found love producing love, joy, reconciliation, fasting, family priorities, Mass being the center of our life, the rosary, prayer, and fidelity to the things most important to our state in life. These are precisely what the Blessed Mother is asking for throughout the world. At the major sites her plea is conversion. She is the Mediatrix and Advocate for our age, interceding on behalf of mankind; just as she has done for centuries.

Her message has not changed in all of history and the consistency of what she has been saying is startling.

Her titles of Theotokos, Perpetual Virginity, The Immaculate Conception, and The Assumption have all been established as Church Dogma. Each time a Dogma has been proclaimed it has been a fight in the Church. Doctors of the Church have not wanted Dogmas proclaimed. Saints Thomas Aquinas, Catherine of Siena, and Bernard of Clairvaux were not in favor of the Dogma of the Immaculate Conception being proclaimed. The debates start and nothing is accomplished because it is the decision of one person only—the Vicar of Christ. No one else on earth has the ability to make that decision. The Dogma of Coredemptrix, Mediatrix, and Advocate again produce heated debates.

Those who see the need for the Dogma seem to have a greater mystical understanding of the times in which we live. They are the people who have been to places like Medjugorje, and know of Father Gobbi, familiar with the messages of Fatima, Akita, and Amsterdam. These sites are the signposts which point the last several generations on the right spiritual path. These places have interpreted the signs in our midst and made sense. These are the sources of private revelation, which have illumined our path so we may be guided to make the best decisions. In this great age of apostasy these places have been the lighthouse for the stormy seasons. They have been the booster shots and hypodermic needles to spur us on as we are a wayward generation. The life in the Church over the last twenty plus years is in the Cenacles of Father Gobbi and other similar activities.

We have a de facto schism in the Church today and the Dogma will make it official as lines will be drawn in the sand. There will be no more false neutrality. Abortion will be black and white as will fidelity to the Magisterium, the True Presence and a host of other doctrinal issues. We will have to stand on one side or the other of the line as the turtle on the fence post is no longer an option. The Church is entering a new Dark Age and before every Easter Sunday is a Good Friday. The Church will suffer and be purified for only then will it be suitable to meet its bride. The remnant few will go underground and valid Masses will be difficult to find. There will be attempts to extinguish and abolish the Eucharist. The Cenacles will be a source of life and the refuge will be in the Sacred and Immaculate Heart. It is foolish to look elsewhere. Father Gobbi and others have been about formation. A marathoner would never think of running the 26-mile race unless there were proper training. This is why the messages of Father Gobbi lasted twenty-five years. Where we have been headed has been told to us in great detail. People from all languages and cultures following the messages are able to finish each other's sentences and are expecting similar events to take place in the near future.

Why do some know this and others not? There is most certainly an element of grace as well as free will.

It's because some people have been tracking with the information given by the Blessed Mother as it has been dispensed like never before in history. There is a fear by many to be associated with the material for fear of being labeled extreme or intellectually inferior so therefore they have missed out on the grace given. The cultural darts sent the way of the believer is often more than some can withstand. But then again, at the foot of the cross was only one apostle.

The word 'co' as in coredemptrix is the biggest problem for Catholics and non-Catholics alike. It simply means "with." "A Woman with the Redeemer." Nothing in divinity is lost, nor is she trying to muscle into the Trinity. Therefore when the terms Coredemptrix, Mediatrix, and Advocate are part of the final Dogma in the Church, there will be those who get it and those who don't, just like every other time in history. And for those who fight it, the choice will be theirs. However, Margaret Mary Alacoque was private revelation that became accepted, Rue du Bac was private revelation that became accepted and flourishes to this day, having given us the Miraculous Medal. She came standing on the globe offering the world graces. 'The Virgin of the Globe' was her title thus showing her role in these calamitous years. The apparitions of Guadalupe, LaSalette, Fatima, Akita, have all been accepted after some stern messages were given to the world with vast numbers of people reluctant to accept them. Sister Faustina's messages were banned outright by the Church, mostly due to poor translation and were opened and promoted by John Paul II at different stages of his priestly life. The Holy Spirit continues to move ahead and those wishing to join the parade are welcome. Those fighting the process will miss the understanding and the graces that come in the given age, "for the Holy Spirit will move where He chooses."

The Dogma will be a defining moment in Church history. As the Blessed Mother was ushered into the upper room and was in the middle of the fearful apostles after the death and Resurrection of Christ, only then was Pentecost. Only then did the fire descend. When she is given her place for the crowning of the Dogma, again there will be a flood of grace to the world with graces that have never been seen before because it is about a New Era of Peace coming to the world. A New Era in the Church will begin in a mystical way. It will be the fulfillment of the promise of Fatima, "In the end my Immaculate Heart will triumph." It will be the fulfillment of the Woman Clothed with the Sun stepping on the head of the serpent. And that is precisely what the entire Marian Movement has been about; a prelude to this great event, that Scripture and saints of old and new have promised to come.

TED FLYNN

Icon of Jesus

Icon of the Blessed Mother and Jesus

Saint Maximilian Kolbe

Saint Francis

Padre Pio

Blessed Mother at Marmora, Canada

Saint Michael

Angel of Children of Purity

Baby Jesus and the New Testament

Guardian Angel

Angel of Goodness

Our Savior Jesus Christ

Saint Raphael

Angel of American History

The Fifteen Promises of Mary to Christians Who Recite the Rosary:

1. Whoever shall faithfully serve me by the recitation of the rosary, shall receive signal graces.

2. I promise my special protection and the greatest graces to all those who shall recite the rosary.

3. The rosary shall be a powerful armor against hell, it will destroy vice, decrease sin, and defeat heresies.

4. It will cause virtue and good works to flourish; it will obtain for souls the abundant mercy of God; it will withdraw the hearts of men from the love of the world and its vanities, and will lift them to the desire of eternal things. Oh, that souls would sanctify themselves by this means.

5. The soul which recommends itself to me by the recitation of the rosary, shall not perish.

6. Whoever shall recite the rosary devoutly, applying himself to the consideration of its sacred mysteries shall never be conquered by misfortune. God will not chastise him in His justice, he shall not perish by an unprovided death; if he be just he shall remain in the grace of God, and become worthy of eternal life.

7. Whoever shall have a true devotion for the rosary shall not die without the sacraments of the Church.

8. Those who are faithful to recite the rosary shall have during their life and at their death the light of God and the plenitude of His graces; at the moment of death they shall participate in the merits of the saints in paradise.

9. I shall deliver from purgatory those who have been devoted to the rosary.

10. The faithful children of the rosary shall merit a high degree of glory in heaven.

11. You shall obtain all you ask of me by the recitation of the rosary.

12. All those who propagate the holy rosary shall be aided by me in their necessities.

13. I have obtained from my Divine Son that all the advocates of the rosary shall have for intercessors the entire celestial court during their life and at the hour of death.

14. All who recite the rosary are my sons, and brothers of my only son Jesus Christ.

15. Devotion of my rosary is a great sign of predestination.

As given to Saint Dominic
Imprimatur: Patrick J. Hayes
Archbishop of New York

Messages For The World

JANUARY 13, 1996

Our heavenly mother said: "My dear children, soon you will see your hearts and souls as God sees them, and as I see them. This will be a time of much confusion and frustration. This is how Satan will try and deceive you into believing that a false peace has come to the world: he will try and convince my children that there is no need to pursue your conversion to God. This is where you, my chosen children, must be ready to do combat with the enemy and take control of my children's souls.

Please, my son, help your heavenly mother with all my children. Always keep focused on my Son, Jesus Christ, and His Cross. The evil head of the Anti-Christ will surface after this enlightenment of souls. My children will then see all of Hell released upon the Earth, and the final battle for souls.

My dear children, you must *always* carry your Rosaries and scapulars. Use your holy water frequently. Pray my children, pray for all your heavenly mother's gentleness. Wisdom and understanding will be needed and a complete trust in my Son, Jesus Christ. Your angels in Heaven will surround you during these times. Call upon them often to pray with you.

Your hope, trust and faith will be rewarded when the new dawn comes. This time will be short, but much devastation will befall the Earth. Remember my children, I love you and will keep those who remain faithful to me under my mantle of love.

Come to me, my children, and let me love and nourish you with my motherly love."

FEBRUARY 13, 1996

Our heavenly mother said: "My beloved children, I am as a river of light from which my Son, Jesus Christ's Light passes to all my children. It pleases me to be honored and venerated as the Immaculate Conception, the Immaculate One of God, and the Mediatrix between my Son, Jesus Christ, and man. Come, my children, and pray with me.

It will be necessary for all to have the greatest faith in my Son's promises. The power of the Father to save His world and His people is absolute and will *not* be overcome by any other power. When the amount of evil has reached the appointed measure, the love of my Immaculate Heart and the Sacred Heart of my Son, Jesus Christ, will burst upon the world to defeat all who stand in the way of the Triumph of Our Two Hearts.

The Trinity of God is given glory, honor and praise each time you, my children, are obedient, each time you defer to the Will of the Father, each time you graciously agree to wait just a little longer for His Will to be done in your life. Much faith, trust and hope are needed, my children, in order to survive the chastisements which await you. In the coming year, you shall see an ever-increasing number of natural disasters, wars, and famine. Your prayers are needed to receive graces at this time, when they will be most needed. All is about to unfold in your presence.

The battle looms fiercely. Feelings of oppression and distraction will result from the major events in Satan's plan to conquer the world. My dear children, you have fallen victim to His deceit and cunning ways. My Enemy causes much confusion in my children and leads them to seek happiness and pleasure in the sensual things of the world. Remember, my children, as my Son, Jesus Christ, has taught you: store all your treasures in *heaven*.

Dear children, the Father, like all good fathers, in His Mercy and Love will need to punish, to chastise those of you who are rebellious and *refuse* to acknowledge my Son, Jesus Christ. For even as I speak, many of my children have been condemned to Hell through their own actions. The world of the Evil One has convinced them that *evil* is the way to pleasure, holiness, peace and happiness. No, I tell you, it is only through my *Son*, Jesus Christ, and the acceptance of His divine Will, will you, my children, ever come to know Love, Peace, Happiness and Holiness.

Pray my children, *pray*, for my children who ignore the signs from Heaven and refuse to accept the truth. Unless you say 'yes' to my Son's invitation, nothing, *nothing*, my children, can and will ever be accomplished in your lives. Accept and *trust* in the mystery of God's love.

My children, *listen* to your heavenly mother and strive to be in complete and total submission to my Son's Will. It is the *only* hope and solace you will have in the future months ahead of you. Practice always your total consecration to me, the Immaculate One. Come with me, my dear children, and you will see the joy at the end, living with me and my Son, Jesus Christ, in a paradise and in Heaven.

I love all my children so *much*. Please accept my invitation and follow me to Eternal Salvation."

MARCH 13, 1996

Our heavenly mother said: "My children, you must learn to honor God and listen to His Commandments until the Earth is cleansed of sin. There will be much weeping and gnashing of teeth.

I weep tonight in much sorrow, for many of my children are lost. Many of my children will die because of the great destruction, and those who have been worthy to me and trust in me will be purified in the fires of Purgatory.

These times are *most* serious, and I, your heavenly mother, am calling you to unity in prayer of petition to the Father. He is greatly saddened for the need of this punishment.

The end of time, my children, is very near, and my Son, Jesus Christ, calls and invites you to accept His invitation, but with a very heavy Heart.

Come back to me, my beloved children, the time is short and I can no longer hold back the hand of the Father.

Dear ones, I, your mother, in much sorrow weep this night for the benefit of your souls. Please listen closely to my words. They are given as a pure gift from the Father who has made us. His great Fatherly love for us is meant to make us comfortable in His Presence.

In these times of terrible confusion with my children, each of you must accept the Divine Plan that you are being lead to, for my Son, Jesus Christ, directs every action around you for good which will bring you more closely to Him and away from the darkness, sadness and coldness, for which many of my children live.

Read my Son's holy words in Scripture every day and receive His precious Body and Blood. It is only through this and prayers will the Holy Spirit enlighten you as to the meaning of what I am telling you. Unless you say yes to my Son's invitation, nothing in your lives will ever be accomplished, for many of my children pray for their own desires and pleasures.

Remember you were created through no choice of your own, but you will not be saved without choices that you will make.

The outcome of prayer and obedience is Holiness, Happiness and Peace. The fruits of virtue are born by the spirit of my children who choose to dwell in the garden of the Father's Will. Without this, my children, you will be lost forever.

You will see, my children, as you accept my Son's invitation and travel the journey, it will lead you to Him and His Will and away from what Satan would have you believe as being the joy, happiness and love of your current world.

Satan is now at his most powerful time and leads many of my children through temptation to eternal Hell. Be strong my children, do *not* be deceived. And persevere to the Eternal Salvation of my Son's Kingdom. When your faith is weak, pray to the Holy Spirit to strengthen your faith and then trust, live in hope, and have faith in me, your heavenly mother.

My love is yours, my children. I will always love my children who have trusted my truth and have and continue to remain faithful to me."

APRIL 13, 1996

Our heavenly mother said: "Dear children, today like never before, I call you to pray for peace, for peace in your hearts, peace in your families and peace in the whole world. Satan wants wars and the lack of peace. He wants to destroy all which is good. Please pray, pray, *pray*, my children, the Rosary. It is your protection and salvation. Only through prayer will you be completely mine and I shall be able to help you.

Draw your strength from my Son and Lord, Jesus Christ, and from His mighty power. Receive Him each day in the Holy Eucharist. For it is through the Holy Eucharist will you receive the protection of God so that you may stand firm against the temptations of Satan.

My dear children, please pray, for your country will be so devastated before long. You will see bloodshed like your country has never known. It will be many years before a return to peace and the world will be decimated to an incredible degree. In preparation for this time you will no longer have the Holy Eucharist on your altars. Fortify yours through prayer and in my Immaculate Heart.

Praise my Son and adore His Holy Majesty, as we wait together for the hour to strike. All is in readiness, devastation and destruction are soon to be the norm.

Spend all your time, my children, in the light, while time and light remain. There is much joy in Heaven for all the good that will be done from the destruction and cleansing. As my motherly appearances all over the world come to an end, great doubt and confusion will enter into many of my children. Satan will use this time to deepen the confusion and cause much panic. My army in Heaven is ready, and waits for the Father's sign to go into battle.

I speak these words to you, my children, to calm your hearts so that when you see events begin you will be strong and calm. Please, my children, go to Confession each week and repent. This will help purify yourselves. Those who remain faithful to me and my Son, Jesus Christ will be protected in my mantle. Many of my children will be brought to Heaven to pray for those remaining on Earth.

You must surrender yourself totally to the Father's design for your life and feel total peace. **Remember, my children, that nothing is more important to you as the time spent in greater communion with my Son and His desires and words for you.**

My dear ones, you would not believe all the secret plans that are in place to dominate the world by those who are enemies of God. Crimes against my children cannot continue to go unchecked by the Justice of God.

The youth who belong to me will be preserved for the future Church, in order for it to continue to flourish.

The Golden Age of Peace and purity that is about to become a reality during the Triumph of my Immaculate Heart will be filled with those who preserve to the end. Always believe that you will be protected in my mantle of love.

Go in peace for now, and please continue to hold my hand and *pray*, my dear, dear children."

MAY 13, 1996

Our heavenly mother said: "My dearest children of the world, I, your Mother, the Immaculate Virgin Mother of my Son, Jesus Christ, am here to tell you of my endearing and everlasting love for each of you. Loved ones, you are all so dear to me and I watch over each of you in the tenderest of fashions. You are protected, if you wish, under my mantle and in the refuge of my Immaculate Heart.

There will soon be things happening in the world which you will not understand nor comprehend. It will be very hard to justify, at times, love in all you will see and in all you will experience. But there is a great Love and Mercy that is to transpire in each of you for the good of all the children of God.

My children, please accept my plea of mercy and stop denying my truth for which I have and will foretell you. I, your Mother, cannot change you in your thinking, for only you can do this by accepting my invitations. I can only invite you, for I know what is best for you, my children. I cannot and will not interfere in your free will, but can urge you to reconsider how it works in your lives.

I will supply you always with the necessary tools that you will need for today and tomorrow. **I, your Mother, am pleading with you most urgently, most lovingly, children, to accept my words, for the time is *short*.**

Pray to the Holy Spirit to open up your hearts and souls. There is not now, and will not be in the future, any room for confusion or fear. Fear or confusion of any kind is not from Heaven, but from Satan. Only love is from God. That is why I am manifesting my deep love for you, my children.

Please accept your Mother's love, for you will receive the graces to cast out all confusion and fear, but you must want and call upon me, my dear children. *Trust* in your heavenly mother, for I weep in much sorrow, in knowing that many of my children do not accept my words because of the pains it brings them. For they are lost and confused in a world controlled by Satan and wish not to leave it, but remain victims to His temptations.

Come to me, my children, for consolation and protection and accept the Holy Spirit for guidance and the graces to live the Divine Plan my Son, Jesus Christ, has done for you.

I love you deeply and enfold you into my motherly arms and kiss each of you most tenderly. I am and will always be a prayer away. Come to me, my children, let me love and nourish you and fill you with my motherly love.

I love you my children, I *love* you my children!"

JUNE 13, 1996

Our heavenly mother said: **"My beloved children, it is most important that you now have your hearts ready. Prepare them every morning and evening through prayer, for my Son's Coming is very near. Only the Father knows when, but all of Heaven is preparing.**

I, your Mother, am now urgently telling you to seriously prepare to wait and be ready for my Son's reign and the Triumph of my Immaculate Heart over Satan. My children you will bear witness to what I am saying. Please do *not* put off repentance.

There is much confusion and chaos in the world today caused by Satan, and an ever-increasing darkness surrounding mankind. This is tragic, my children, for you have fallen victim to his temptations. Please my children, give me your souls and hearts; I will keep them in my love, and caress each as a very special child of mine. I love you, my children, very much.

Before you see my Son's glorious return, our Father will show His merciful Justice, because of His infinite Love for His children. His Love will give my children a chance to come into His arms where He will embrace and love you, my children, like never before. When the Father gives you the final opportunity of choosing Heaven or hell, you will then, my children, choose your fate through your own free will, your free choice.

The Father and my Son, Jesus Christ, will invite you into the Heavenly Kingdom. I, your mother, weep in much sorrow for many of my children have turned their backs to my Son, and He will turn His back on many of my children forever.

The time has come for you, my children, to make the most serious decisions in your lives, the decision of an eternity of

happiness and love or an eternity filled with tears and regret. **My children, my Triumph is here and is continuing in the hearts and souls of my children who acknowledge me. What** *joy***, my children, you will feel and have when you see my Son, Jesus Christ, come into His glory! But only after the very turbulent times that must precede His Second Coming.**

Be strong, my children. *Trust* in my Son, have *faith* in my Son and *hope* in my Son's Mercy for my children's sins. My children, all my teaching must be taken to heart, learned, studied and put into holy action, for you will be guided by the Holy Spirit at all times. Have a deep conviction of love, my little ones, a total confidence in my love and care for you. This will be your Peace.

Live in my peace, my children, to see clearly the state of the sinfulness existing in each soul that will cause many of my children to panic. My children are not aware of the sinful lives they are living, for Satan has deceived many of my children. The revelation of this state of sinfulness will become a source of bitterness and great sorrow to many of my children who have fallen victim to Satan.

I have pleaded with the Father to allow me to gather my children under my mantle, but I am in sorrow in knowing that the time has ended in delaying the Father's hand of Justice. Please ponder these words, my children, you must believe them completely. I am your mother who loves you.

Hear my plea, my children!"

JULY 13, 1996

Our heavenly mother said: **"My beloved children, my Son is coming; know and believe that this is true! The Earth must be cleansed in order for my Son to fulfill the Scriptures before His triumphant return. All that is written in Scripture will be fulfilled.** My children will be witnesses to these great events I have foretold you. Satan is at war against the Father. He wishes to destroy the world and return it to a state of chaos to which he was cast by the Father. That is why sinful people who follow Satan wish only to destroy goodness and beauty and return to darkness.

Now is the time for the Triumph of my Immaculate Heart to begin, as the darkness becomes nearly complete. Without your mother, my children will be lost and remain uncertain the way to turn. Without the touch of your mother's hand, my children's hearts will grow cold. Please, my children, follow me; learn and grow in the virtues of goodness. I will defeat the Evil One with my cohort of angels, my heavenly angels, who love me and have given their lives to my cause.

A new Heaven and new Earth are about to be born. O, alien world, you have drifted far from the path of salvation and have become a foreigner in your own land. You are not aware of and have forgotten your birthright purchased for you, my children, by my Son. All is about to be purified and rendered clean in the sight of God. Then it will be deemed worthy to present it to my Son, upon His return. My Son will, in turn, take all to His Father and They will rejoice together over the good fortune. Happy and blessed are my children who will see this day.

Give praise to the Father Who so loves the world that He will send His only Son, Our Lord Jesus Christ, again to save His people and bring all to the completion of this age. The future, my children, of all who pray the Rosary and follow me is bright with the light of my Son, Jesus Christ.

Be filled with joy, my children, as you work with me for the goodness of mankind. Be filled with gratitude to the Father for allowing me, your heavenly mother, the extended time of grace to teach my beloved children.

I love you, my children, and will always keep my children, who are dear to my Immaculate Heart, under the protection of my mantle.

Please accept the Truth for which I speak, and pray, pray, pray my children! I love you all so very much."

AUGUST 13, 1996

Our heavenly mother said: "My son, the Anti-Christ will use many deceitful devices to mislead and capture souls. My Son, Jesus, has told you that He will confuse the proud and raise the lowly. You will see my powers in action, so that I will protect many of my faithful children from Satan. This is a hopeful protection that I offer my children in prayer, who follow my Son's Will. You will see miraculous things happening through my angels.

My children, your sins are scorching the Earth with evil, as the lifeblood of your faith is being tested. Your chastisements on the land will force people to move to new lands. Your current farms are suffering droughts and floods as never witnessed before. Soon growing food will be difficult and it will be desperately needed. My children, you have been turned into evil waters that are leading you away from my Son, Jesus Christ.

My children, you will soon perish in the hands of the Evil One. I keep sending you many messages to awaken the spirit.

graces that will lead you to Eternal Salvation.

In order for my Son's Purification of the Earth to be effective, there must be dramatic changes. When you see these changes, brace yourselves, my children, for my Son's Warning, which will be a startling experience to see your entire life in judgment. My children, I bring you this message of hope, even amidst the adversity now around you. Heed the meaning of this Warning and change your life before it is too late to be saved. Believe me that I am with you always, ready to protect and help you prepare.

Whatever happens will be the direct result of the Father's Love and Mercy for all mankind. Do not worry about yourselves. Just remember, the King of Glory is returning to secure His victory for His people. Just as I have prepared myself and everything necessary to bring my Son, Jesus Christ, into the world, so now the Father is sending me to my children to prepare them to receive Him."

SEPTEMBER 13, 1996

Our heavenly mother said: "My children, you are witnessing an experience when I, your Mother, will triumph in the defeat of Satan. After my Triumph, I will usher in an Era of Peace that has been promised even in Scripture. I have told you many wonderful things that you will experience in this time that will be free of evil. Do not doubt how my glory will be carried out, but rejoice in my love, as you are brought closer to Heaven than ever before. Those who are faithful, and live through the tribulation, will have their reward.

Do not be concerned over the details of how my Son's Will will be done. It is my keeping with Scripture and my promises that

Do not be concerned over the details of how my Son's Will will be done. It is my keeping with Scripture and my promises that are more importantly heard. Be joyful in my gifts to you and do not doubt over anything I have given you. I give you all reason to be joyful and your thanks should be ever in your prayers.

My dear children, today is such a special one in your lives and mine. **We stand on the brink of a New Era, consecrated and committed totally to the Divine Will of the Father in Heaven.** You are all so very dear to my Immaculate Heart, my dearest little ones. I am so in love with each of you with a tender mother's heart. I am being allowed to come into your world and be seen by many of His special messengers. Because of His Second Coming, my dear Son, Jesus Christ, has allowed me to speak to very many of my faithful children, so that you may all benefit from my words of warning and love and preparedness.

Each time you feel panic and confusion, focus on my Son, Jesus, and your Mother. Ask to be reunited to Our Hearts and be allowed to concentrate again on the truth and the reality of all that is.

Please, my children, seek comfort and refuge in my arms. Know that Jesus and I long to hold and comfort you. It is very important that you continue to seek our Lord's Love. This Love will be a healing for your soul and will strengthen my children for the End Times. The Love of my Son is the most powerful force on Earth. Please ponder these words. You must believe them completely.

I am your Mother who loves you. Please hear my plea."

OCTOBER 13, 1996

Our heavenly mother said: **"My son, as the time of Purification comes upon you, you will be stripped of your possessions and creature comforts. You may complain that these chastisements are too severe, but if you had to purify the Earth as my Son's Justice demands, you could no more deal with this scope of evil.**

Trust in my Son, that what He does has an overall saving grace, which man, in his weakness, cannot fully understand. His Will be done, and my love will shine forth on the just.

The wicked will be brought to suffer for their crimes, as a Reign of Peace will come over the land. In order to follow me, you must give your life over to your Mother, so you can daily nourish and refresh your faith. Only my faithful will be brought back to life with glorified bodies. My children who are faithful will be purified and enjoy their reward in splendor with our Lord, Jesus Christ.

My dear, dear children, can you see, my little ones, how the natural disasters have been increased all over the world, as well as wars and diseases? There is much apostasy in my Church, the very Church my Son gave to all His children. Please pray for my beloved Church and priests. I love them so. Live the Gospel and live according to the teachings of my Church. Your prayers, fasts, vigils, and sacrifices will help things according to Heaven's plan.

This is a time of battle between good and evil. Invoke St. Michael and His angels and your guardian angels. The Rosary will be your weapon, as well as the scapular your shield. Listen to me, your Mother, and always hold the Rosary and pray, Pray, *pray*, my children! If you could only see the pestilence and disease that will soon spread throughout the world, as waters rise, buildings collapse, crops devastated beyond salvaging, there will be much hunger and much suffering, much horror and devastation that has not been seen or felt like this ever before.

Each day continue to consecrate yourselves to your Mother, this is your only hope. Your sign, the sign of my heart, on each of your foreheads and hearts, will become your saving grace which will counter the sign of the Beast.

Pray with me, and never let go of my hand. As your trust in me grows, so shall your faith in my Son, Jesus. You, yourselves, will die completely, as He lives more and more in you through me. Do all for His honor and glory."

NOVEMBER & DECEMBER 1996: No Messages

JANUARY 13, 1997

Our heavenly mother said: "My dear children, please accept your mother's invitation to external Happiness, Love and Peace. Today is a time of trial. Many of my children will be confused to what they will see and hear. Many will refuse to accept my words because of their denial and hardened hearts. The Evil One is out in a very strong force causing many of my children to become confused. This is how Satan works, for He is the Master of Deceit, very cunning and extremely shrewd. This is where you, my children, must be prepared to reject and confront the enemy and take control of your souls.

Please, my children, remain focused on the Cross, follow and accept my Son's invitations. I can not change you or your thinking. Only my children can do this for themselves. I can not interfere in your free will. I plead for you, my children, most urgently, most lovingly, to take my words and receive them into your hearts. For only those of my

children who accept my Son's invitation will live the Peace, Love and Happiness of Life. This does not mean that all will be saved from suffering and dying for their Faith. Hardships may begin at any moment and I beg you to remain in prayer and receive the graces my Son offers through His invitation.

My children must realize that their decisions will depend on their own free will. As you become more purified, the temptations of Satan will become much stronger, but always remain faithful to me and trust in my Son, Jesus Christ. I your Mother weep in much sorrow for many of my children who are weak and continue to deny the truth and remain confused in a sea of confusion caused by my adversary.

Dear children, I, your Mother of Sorrows, speak this night for the benefit of your hearts and souls. For many of my children's souls will be lost into Hell for eternity. Please listen closely to my words, for they are given as a gift from the Father. **His great Fatherly love for us is meant to make us comfortable in His Divine Presence, to relax in the warmth of His care and wonderful providence of our very lives.**

In these times of terrible chaos, confusion and destruction of my children's lives by Satan, each of my children need more than ever to know and accept my Son's invitation and Divine Plan. For my Son directs every action around you for your good, to bring you most quickly and closely to Him.

I love you, my children, deeply, and enfold you in my motherly arms and kiss each of you most tenderly now and always. I am and will always be a prayer away.

Come to me, my children, let me love and nourish you and fill you with my Son's Love, Peace, understanding and blessings.

I love you, my children. I *love* you, my children. I will *always* love you my children!"

FEBRUARY 13, 1997

Our heavenly mother said: "**My children, soon the time will come when you will no longer have the opportunity to visit my Son, Jesus Christ in His Churches or seek peace before Him in the Sacrament of the altar.** You will no longer hear my voice or see me. Many of my children, especially my chosen children's hearts, will be saddened and heavy. Remember, they must be filled with faith and hope in their Father in Heaven, just like my Son, Jesus Christ, Who died on the cross for our sins, only to be brought to life by the Father and have Eternal Salvation in Heaven.

There will come a time soon when the children of God will go through persecutions for my Son, Jesus Christ. This will be a time of great suffering, for the feeling of abandonment will be very present in the world. Hearts will look about in terror for a safe place to go. Woe to those of my children who refuse my truth and seek the meaningless pleasure of the world! They walk and live in darkness. They have no love, peace or happiness in their lives. To understand the mysteries of Heaven more fully, my children must unite themselves to me, your heavenly mother. The more fully you surrender yourself to me and my Son, Jesus Christ, the more you will know who We are.

Every day you must spend time in quiet prayer and become filled with the grace and holiness of my Son. He is the Lord of Mercy, praised by the Father for His Divine Plan for the salvation of His children.

My children, my love is always with you, as is my heart. Bring me your impatience and thoughts of discouragement. Hide within me from the hatreds of the world. Surrender, my children, completely your free will to my Son, Jesus Christ. By doing so, your soul will unite itself more readily to my Son's Divine Will. This is when the soul no longer cares to exercise it's own free will, but rather to return to the Will of the Creator of Heaven and Earth, your Heavenly Father. And when your soul, my child, is in the state of sanctifying grace, it is like a radiant jewel which has gained the Kingdom of Heaven on Earth. It is here, my children, that the Most Holy Trinity wants to dwell at all times. Always give praise to the Father, the Son and the Holy Spirit.

My love is yours, my dear children, please accept it and let me hold you close to me.

I love you, my children. I love you, my children. I will always love you my children!"

MARCH 13, 1997

Our heavenly mother said: "My little ones, when you have finished your day and before going on to the next, please stop and give thanks to your Father in Heaven. Gratitude is a necessary ingredient on your way to holiness. Appreciating God's gifts will help you, my children, realize what a privilege it is to be allowed to serve your Father in Heaven. All that we have has been given to us by God and without His Presence at every moment in our lives, my children, you would have nothing and be nothing.

The very act by which you were created, by Love from the Father, calls you to love as my Son Jesus Christ has loved. The very Love which sustains and nourishes you, calls you to love everyone.

The destructive forces of evil which exist today cannot be allowed to continue. The Father has decreed to me, your heavenly mother, that there has been enough suffering by all my children. The cleansing power of the Father's love, His Divine Son, Jesus Christ, will rid the world of all evil that is not of Love. I weep in much sorrow and pain in knowing that many of my children will be cast into Hell and eternal darkness.

My Son's Heart bleeds with much pain in rejecting His people who have accepted the way of the Evil One. But I assure you, my children, that His Mercy is just, and His Justice can see the souls of *all* His people.

My children, a time is approaching when the Earth will be shaken by the heavenly powers. Devastation will not only change the face of the Earth, but claim many of my children to their final hour.

Please pray, my children, the Rosary every day. Pray not only for salvation of your souls, but for others, as well. Receive the Body of my Son, Jesus Christ, daily, to nourish your thirst of Love. Receive His Divine Plan that He has made for you, for the time is very short to which I, your Mother, am forewarning you. **When these events occur, the time for your salvation will be too late for conversion**.

Please, my dear children, *accept* my invitation and follow your heavenly mother to a new Earth, which my Son, Jesus Christ will walk, for Heaven and Earth will become one. I will pour out my love to you always, my children, and always intercede for you with my Son, Jesus Christ, and lead my children to the path of holiness that leads to Eternal Life."

APRIL 1997 - No Message

MAY 13, 1997

Our heavenly mother said: "My dear children, time is *short*! There is soon to come much of what has been foretold you in Scripture. The Earth will be punished with all kinds of plagues and wars. The Ten Kings will be allied to the Anti-Christ and be the only ruler of the world.

The Earth is at the beginning of its pain and will die, a prey of terror and anguish caused by Satan. There will be famine and contagious diseases, rain of hail storms that will destroy cities, earthquakes, and fire from Heaven will fall. The whole world will be struck with *terror*, for many of my children have been seduced by Satan and his pleasures, and do not adore my Son, Jesus Christ, Who lived among them.

You must prepare by spiritually focusing on the condition of your souls and my Son's Second Coming. You will then see the Reign of Two Hearts, the Triumph of my Immaculate Heart and the Reign of the Sacred Heart of Jesus.

To the unbelievers and those who have refused my truth and live in a false world of 'happiness' and pleasure, it will be *very* frightening. Much prayer and fasting is needed.

My Son, Jesus Christ, as King, must be prayed to, adored and honored. Please pray for unity. This is the 11th hour of Grace and Mercy and it is IMPERATIVE to increase prayer.

I urge you, my children, to practice the following immediately:

- Try to attend Mass daily.
- Go to confession weekly.
- Always keep your souls in a state of Divine Grace.
- Receive the Holy Eucharist daily, the true Body and Blood of my Son.
- Pray the Rosary and Chaplet of Mercy daily.

My children, you must live each day as if it were your *last*. Faith, trust, love and conversion all through prayer, for only through prayer will you have Peace and purity of heart, mind and soul.

I weep in much, much sorrow for my children who live in confusion caused by Satan. They enjoy the false pleasures of a world controlled by evil. They refuse my truth and my Son's Divine Plan.

These are very serious times, my children, where confusion cannot be accepted and your hearts confused as to the direction to follow. Remember the Truth runs *always* to God.

In the coming days, many will see the truth of their hearts and souls. You will need to surrender totally the remainder of your lives on Earth to my Son, rather than your own desires.

Open your hearts to receive all the graces and power you will ever need, my dear ones. I love you with all the love that could be poured out for you. You can feel my love if you want to, if you would only stop and *listen* to my words. Please *believe* these words, my children, they are only meant to save you from final damnation into Hell.

I love you my children, and will protect those who have *listened* to my truth and followed me."

JUNE 13, 1997

Our heavenly mother said: "My dear children,

The time has *come*, my children, for the deliverance from the slavery of sin and evil. Please be warned of the *shortness* of time.

Pray, my children. *Pray*, my children! Pray the Rosary daily, for the Wrath of God will *soon* descend upon mankind!

The Father is saddened, and my Immaculate Heart weeps by the need for this punishment, for this Purification is needed, for many of my children have fallen victim and live the Evil One's ways. I can no longer hold back the Father's hand of Vengeance.

Pray for your country. It is in most serious and grave danger. Repent for the sins being committed against God the Father, the Sacred Heart of Jesus Christ, and the Immaculate Heart of your heavenly mother. A judgment will soon fall on all my children. Pray, pray, as you have *never* prayed before, and be filled with the Divine Love of my Son, Jesus Christ.

Soon you will see unbelievable events and wonders, worked by the hand of my Son. Pray for the Holy Spirit to be with you. He will give you the graces necessary for your needs and guide you to the path of holiness.

Have faith, trust and confidence in me, my children. I will protect you under my mantle of love.

Please, my little ones, bring others to the knowledge of my Son through the Sacrament of His Divine Presence on the altar. Receive Him with loving and open hearts. Let your Lord and Savior, Jesus Christ, transform you into His makings.

I am the Mother of All Virtues, and will lead my devoted children into the Kingdom of my Son, to Eternal Salvation. He is the Lord. He is Love. He is the Almighty. He is the Most Holy One.

I love you, my children, and am pleased for you accompanying your heavenly mother on this journey. Always live in my Son's Peace, Love and Mercy.

I love you my children. I love you my children. I love you."

JULY 13, 1997

Our heavenly mother said: "My dear children, today is a special day in your life and mine. **We stand on the brink of a New Era, consecrated and committed totally to the Divine Will of Our Father in Heaven. My Son, Jesus Christ, is about to return to the Earth on which He was born 2000 years ago. Through the grace of the Father, I am preparing you to receive Him for His triumphant return.**

O, my dearest ones, can you not see that it will be the Love of my Son, Jesus Christ, that will be the cause of the great Victory for justice and peace in the world? Please believe me, my children, He *is* coming! Prepare your houses and your souls. Dress your souls in the finest array of graces, the odor of holiness, and the joy of gladness and rejoicing. Attend to your garments and stay close to me, your heavenly mother, as we make the final plans. A new Heaven and a new Earth are about to be born.

Be warned, my children, that Satan will play upon your pride with his cunning and shrewd ways. The darkness of the soul will invade all of you and your choices will be more difficult. There is no one person on Earth able to fight Satan without the strength of God. Pray, Pray, *pray* always the Rosary, my children, which I have given you. It is not only a weapon against Satan, but the necessary link between Heaven and Earth.

Your own trust and faith will be a beacon for the impetus to faith of all who seek our Lord and Savior, Jesus Christ. Return *now* and bathe yourselves in the waters of grace and forgiveness in frequent confession weekly, and dress your souls with my virtues and the gifts of the Holy Spirit.

My Son's Cross was, and still is, the sign of Love for us. Each of my children must offer up their crosses to Him, and in union with Him, as a sign of love for Him.

Give to me, my children, all your tears of remorse of repentance, asking forgiveness for yourselves and the world, in making reparation to my Son, Jesus Christ.

Please pray together with me, my children, for the coming of the Kingdom. The salvation of the entire world is in the hands of those who *pray*.

I am your heavenly mother, who comes in Love and Peace, to fill all my children. Prepare yourselves each day to be filled with the Grace, Peace and Love of Jesus Christ, our Lord and Savior.

I am your Mother, who *loves* you my children. *Please* hear my call.

I love you, my children. I *love* you, my children. I will *always* love you my children!"

AUGUST 13, 1997

Our heavenly mother said: "My dear children, I call you to the urgency in preparing your hearts and souls, in the advent of the Second Coming into the world of my Son, Jesus Christ. Spend your final days in union with Our Two Hearts and our Heavenly Father's Divine Will for you.

Many signs are being given to you, yet they are ignored because of the deceits of the Evil One.

I am the Mediatrix of All Graces. I take my dear children and prepare their souls so that they are pleasing to my Son, Jesus Christ. You must have a *complete* surrender and consecration to His Mercy and Sacred Heart. Once united to Him, all obstacles to reach Eternal Salvation in Heaven are removed.

Our Lord and Savior, Jesus Christ, is the Truth and the *only* way to Eternal Salvation. Today, I call you to a greater unity with each other and within my Son's Church. Pray, Pray, *pray*, my children, for my beloved priests, bishops and cardinals, that they remain steadfast and obedient to my chosen Pope, who will lead His people into the New Era.

My dear little children, the world today is under much attack by Satan and his cohorts. Many seek to surround themselves with the simple pleasures, instead of placing their treasures in Heaven, where they will reign for eternity with our Lord and Savior Jesus Christ. Always give praise to the Father, the Son, and Holy Spirit. These are the sweetest sounds to ascend into Heaven.

Return *now*, my children, and bathe yourselves with the graces and forgiveness from my Son. Our Lord's Love will heal your souls, and give you needed strength to endure the chastisements which await you.

You will soon see cataclysmic events that will never be understood by mankind, and disruptions of every nation on Earth. Can you not see the warnings that already befell the Earth? Why are my children's hearts so *hardened* and their souls so *cold*? Because they are being deceived by the Evil One.

Pray, pray, *pray*, my children, the Rosary daily. Recite the Divine Mercy, in reverence to my Son and receive His Body, Blood, Soul and Divinity each day to nourish your souls.

Please, my children, have a deep conviction of love and a total confidence in me, your heavenly mother.

I love you, my children. I *love* you, my children. I will *always* love you my children!"

SEPTEMBER 13, 1997

Our heavenly mother said: "My beloved children, seek your heavenly mother and replenish your love under my protection, for the Hour and the Day has come upon the world. **Seek the Peace, for the Peace is the Love of my Son, our Lord and Savior, Jesus Christ, which will sustain you through the End Times.**

My adversary has begun to double his efforts in destroying my children's souls to Eternal Darkness and he will leave no stone unturned in the final battle.

Come to me, my children, and protect yourself under the mantle of my Immaculate Heart. And you will see the Triumph of Two Hearts, my Immaculate Heart and the Sacred Heart of my Son, Jesus Christ.

Do not fall victim to the deceits of Satan and the pleasures of a sensual, meaningless world which inhibits the soul in recognizing and feeling the Love of God the Father.

Kneel and pay reverence to Our Father in Heaven, for He is the Creator of both Heaven and Earth, and seek His strength, Love and Peace, for the day has come when mankind will now experience the darkness of his soul and must make a decision whether to follow my Son, Jesus Christ, or my adversary into darkness.

The cataclysmic events, for which I have foretold you, will begin to escalate in numbers, and the devastation to your country will become greater, for this is necessary for the purification of the world. Those who have remained faithful to me will be saved and lead to Eternal Salvation.

Soon the Anti-Christ, with the powers of Satan, will come into being and my Angels of Heaven will lead the faithful to safe havens. And some of my children will be martyred for

my Son's sake. Pray, Pray, *pray* the Rosary daily, as I have asked you, for it will be your weapon against my adversary. Recite each day the Chaplet of Divine Mercy, in atonement for my Son's death for your Salvation, and receive His precious Body, Blood, Soul and Divinity each day to nourish and strengthen your souls. Remain faithful to me, your heavenly mother, and I shall lead you into a New Era of a new world for which my Son shall walk.

My dear little children, you are so very dear to me, *please* hear my calling, *accept* my messages so that you may prepare your souls for what is about to unfold.

I love you, my children. I *love* you, my children. I will *always* love you my children!"

OCTOBER 13, 1997

Our heavenly mother said: "Oh, my dear little children! *Why* have you rejected your heavenly mother's calling to holiness? As I have foretold you, Satan is working against our Heavenly Father's plan for the salvation of His children and bringing the world back to its former beauty.

My adversary wishes to *destroy* the world, and have it remain in a state of chaos without love, and to remain in darkness.

My children, your country continues to sin in the face of God, in order to attain your own desires. The time has now come for the hand of the Almighty One to fall and His Justice to be served to all His peoples. *Heed* my warnings, and seek and hide in the harbor of my Immaculate Heart.

Major earthquakes, a famine, and world-wide pestilence will cause my children to fall to their knees and ask for forgiveness of God. You shall now see the sins of your souls in the judgment of our Lord and Savior, Jesus Christ.

Confess your sins and repent, visit confession weekly to purify and cleanse your souls of sins through Reconciliation. The time has come for many trials, perils, and changes in your lives, and you must be in a state of Divine Grace to withstand these changes.

The evil head of the Anti-Christ will now rise, and all of Hell will be released on Earth for the final battle of souls.

Remember, my children, to always carry your Rosaries, scapulars and holy water as weapons against my adversary.

Pray, pray, *pray*, my beloved children for yourselves, and your beloved ones. Pray for my beloved Pope, in the battle for my Son's Church. Pray for his continued health and strength against the schisms that continue in the House of God. Pray for my beloved priests, whom Satan is now attacking in order to obtain their souls, for this will be a time of much confusion of mind, heart and soul for my children.

Remember, my dear little children, that the time has come for the Triumph of My Immaculate Heart, as the world becomes enveloped in complete darkness. Humble yourselves and remain obedient to the Divine Will of Our Heavenly Father. Receive our Father's Love, to nourish you and sustain you each day, and love one another as our Lord and Savior, Jesus Christ, loves you.

The earth is about to be cleansed of sin for the Second Coming of My Son, Jesus Christ, and as it has been foretold you in Scripture, and promised you in Scripture, all these events will come to pass, before the Second Coming, of my Son's return to earth.

O, my dear little children, *why* do you reject the signs that are being given to you from Heaven? The disasters that you are witnessing will increase in number, and are meant to open up your eyes and souls in knowing these are from Heaven. You must trust in me, your heavenly mother, for those who do not will not know the way to follow. Humble yourselves and remain obedient to Our Heavenly Father, and present yourself to Our Lord and Savior, Jesus Christ, as innocent children.

Pray, for the outcome of prayer is your road to holiness, and the salvation of your souls.

Blessed are my children who hear my calling, for they shall receive the Divine Mercy of Our Father in Heaven.

I love you, my children. I *love* you, my children. I will *always* love you my children!"

NOVEMBER 13, 1997

Our heavenly mother said: "Oh, my beloved little children, the next few months are very crucial for the survival of your souls. Live each day according to the teachings of my Son's Church. Do not become anxious in your religious decisions, and call in the Holy Spirit to guide you. Consecrate yourselves to my Son, our Lord and Savior Jesus Christ, for this will be your *only* hope, and it will be the sign that the cohorts of my Angels will be looking for.

The road to Heaven is rough, and narrow, and requires much suffering, and, as you see my Son's Mercy turn to Justice, always remember His Love for all His peoples, the same Love that He embraced on the Cross, the same Love in which He shed His Blood for our sins, a Love in which you must embrace in order to endure your crosses and for the adornment of your souls.

My beloved little children, the times for which you await are about to happen, the return of my Son, our Lord and Savior Jesus Christ, and there will be many signs and wonders given to the world, but you must accept and embrace our Heavenly Father's Divine Will, which will lead you to holiness and the birth of a new Earth and Era of Peace. For those who remain in a sensual world of pleasures will be condemned to final damnation into darkness.

Please, my dear little children, *hear* my calling. Pray, Pray, *pray*, my dear little ones, for the chastisements to come quickly and the birth of a new world. The Triumph of my Immaculate Heart and the Reign of the Sacred Heart of my Son, Jesus Christ, has now come.

Please, my dear little children, *accept* my calling and remain close to my Immaculate Heart, as I lead you to our Lord and Savior, Jesus Christ. Always remember that love is of God, and darkness is of Satan. Come follow me, as I lead you into the beauty, love, and peace of my Son, Jesus Christ, and I am always a prayer away.

I love you, my children. I *love* you, my children. I will **always** love you my children!"

DECEMBER 13, 1997

Our heavenly mother said: "Oh, my dear little children, I come today to remind you to remain in the highest state of holiness, for the continuous outpouring of prayers, and to remain in most perfect union with me, your heavenly mother, through the Sacred Heart of my Son, our Lord and Savior, Jesus Christ. I ask for a complete abandonment of self for the sake of our Lord, for what I have foretold you is about to begin.

My dear little children, you must immerse yourself completely in my strength in order to survive the End Times, for only through accepting '...the Father's Will be done...,' will you be able to live out the promises of Scripture.

The truth for which I have spoken will become apparent when all has been accomplished. You must surrender *totally* yourselves to my Son, our Lord and Savior, Jesus Christ, for He shall lead you to the Promised Land.

All my children who have been faithful to me, and I, your heavenly mother, shall lead you to the Day of our Lord. But *why* have many of my children turned their backs to my Son?

Much suffering will come, for Satan will be given the power to fulfill his plan to destroy the world. But the Lion and the sheep shall rejoice in victory over the defeat of the Evil One.

I ask you, my dear little children, to adore my Son each day for one holy hour in adoration, for this will refresh and strengthen your souls, which will be needed to sustain you through the End Times, for this will be your food for your weary hearts. For each breath of love you shall take, shall be for the glory and honor of our Father in Heaven.

Pray, pray, *pray*, my dear little children, with me, your heavenly mother, each day. **Receive His precious Body, Blood, Soul and Divinity in the Holy Eucharist each day for the nourishment of your souls. Frequent confession, weekly, through Reconciliation, and dress your souls in the finest of linens to receive our Heavenly Father's Grace. And before these events are about to begin, Our Heavenly Father's Mercy shall be poured forth, so that man may have the opportunity to return to God.**

My dear little children, you will then be given a choice of accepting our Heavenly Father's Divine Plan, or not, with your own free will. You will make the most important decisions in your life on whether to accept an eternity with Love, happiness, Peace and joy, or an eternity filled with tears, coldness and darkness.

I weep in much sorrow in knowing that many of my children will live in darkness. You must continue to pray that my dear little children will have a greater trust in Love, in their heavenly mother, as I lead them through the End Times in union with my Son, our Lord and Savior, Jesus Christ. May they dwell in the joy, peace and endless love.

Satan can *not* exist in those souls that belong to me, your heavenly mother, but he shall try to cause much confusion and chaos in your lives.

Oh, my dear little children, please hear my words. *Trust* in me, your heavenly mother. Follow me, as I lead you to my Son, our Lord and Savior, Jesus Christ. And humble yourselves as innocent little children.

I will *always* be with you, my dear, dear children. And in the end, I shall triumph in victory with the Sacred Heart of my Son, Jesus Christ.

I love you, my children. I *love* you, my children. I will *always* love you my children!"

JANUARY 13, 1998

Our heavenly mother said: "Oh, my dear little children, I, your heavenly mother, the Immaculate Virgin of the Son of God, love each of you very, very much. I watch over each of you in the tenderest of fashions.

Many things are now happening in your world which many of my children will never come to understand. I am the model to follow on how one must die to oneself, to become little innocent children in the eye of our Lord and Savior, Jesus Christ. Follow Him, focus on His Cross, and trust in Him through the deceptions of the Evil One, for the evil head of the Anti-Christ is about to surface. Have courage and strength to fight the temptations of Satan.

The spirit of Wisdom and Truth shall come to you through the Holy Spirit. It is through the Holy Spirit that you will come to understand the truth and the virtues of life. Humility is the greatest of all virtues. Please, my dear little children, show and teach all my children the virtues that I have taught you. Remember to frequent the Sacraments of Reconciliation weekly and to confess your sins in cleansing your souls. Your soul *must* be in a state of grace in order to have the Love seep into your hearts, into receiving our Lord and Savior, Jesus Christ, in the Era of Peace.

The salvation of the world rests on those who pray. Pray, Pray, *pray*, my dear little children, the Rosary daily, for many will soon experience the illumination of their souls and they will then have to make a decision in accepting Our Heavenly Father's Divine Plan, or rejecting the Mercy and forgiveness of my Son, our Lord and Savior, Jesus Christ.

Your world is about to be purified to its new beginning. *prepare* for the Era of Peace.

Hold onto my hands, dear little children, and walk with me on the road to holiness and let us proclaim the Good Word of our Father in Heaven.

Call upon me often in prayer for my intercession to help you, for I am always a prayer away. Follow the teachings of my Son's Church and receive the Holy Eucharist daily to nourish your hearts and souls.

I love you, my children. I *love* you, my children. I will *always* love you my dear little children!"

FEBRUARY 13, 1998

Our heavenly mother said: "Oh, my dear children, the time has come for the deliverance from the slavery of sin and heresy. You must remain closer to me than ever before, listen to my voice filled with love and concern for all of you.

Oh, my dearest little children, know that Satan ascends to his highest power now. Rely on the Immaculate Heart of your heavenly mother and the Sacred Heart of my Son, Jesus Christ, as your place of refuge. Your ability to fight the persecutions of Satan will be determined by the amount of love that you have for my Son, our Lord and Savior, Jesus Christ. Let my words of love that I have promised from the bliss of Paradise fill you with joyful expectations and conviction.

There are no words to describe the greatest Love, of our Father in Heaven. Become one in union with Him, for the plans that He has for you. The world must be totally devoted and committed to the salvation for all. My Son, Jesus Christ must be prayed to, adored, honored, glorified and become the *center* of your lives.

Now, things will be more and more and more difficult and Satan will try to destroy your faith. My Son's words of Wisdom and Light are a total joy when offered for the glory and honor of our Father in Heaven. The honor of my Son's Truth will be your greatest strength, for the cunning and deceitful ways of the Evil One can *not* prevail against His Truth.

More vessels are needed for the nourishment of my children who starve for the Bread of Life. I, your heavenly mother, will give them an abundance of graces in order to open their hearts and to receiving the Word of God, and these seedlings shall yield an abundance at the time of harvest.

The Day Of The Lord begins with a New Dawn, for it is a time for salvation and co-redeeming each other, for there is little time left for conversion. Soon our Father will grant the graces for mankind to clearly see their sins, for then my children will not be deceived by the lies of the Prince of Darkness, whose powers and illusions confuse my children.

Pray, Pray, *pray*, my dear children! Pray with an outpouring of your hearts to the Divine Doctrine of our Father in Heaven, and know that our Father acts in the best interest of all my children, for all that has been promised to you in Scripture is about to be fulfilled.

It is only through the guidance of the Holy Spirit that you shall be led through these very serious and trying times. Prepare yourselves, my children, for the events that are about to unfold. Have faith and trust in my Son, Jesus Christ. Hold my hand as I keep you close to my Immaculate Heart and under the protection of my mantle, as I lead my faithful children to the Day Of The Lord.

I love you, my children. I *love* you, my children. I will *always* love you my children!"

MARCH 13, 1998

Our heavenly mother said: "Oh, my dearest little ones, in this the time of Lent unite yourselves to my Son, Jesus Christ, through penance and fasting. The day and the hour are upon the world. These are glorious times that you are living, a time for preparation. Kneel in readiness and be prepared for all that is about to come. And, as you become purified, your convictions will become stronger through faith, and through prayer your convictions will become greater. It is a time to ask for forgiveness for one's sins and to confess them to our Lord and Savior, Jesus Christ, for His Mercy knows no boundaries.

Many of my children need to know how Mercy works, by practicing forgiveness in their lives. Come to me, my dear children, in humility, obedience and a complete trust in your heavenly mother. This is a time for strengthening and reassurance of faith and trust.

Satan will not make you rest in these the End Times. He will try to convince you that your efforts are fruitless in trying to reconcile with God. The influence of the Evil One can only be countered through God's infinite Graces and Mercy.

A new-dawn day will come to those who remain faithful to my Son, Jesus Christ. To be in a state of sanctifying grace is a treasure in which the soul stands in the sight of our Heavenly Father, Whose Peace is a result of the total abandonment to the Heavenly Divine Plan.

Beauty reigns in the garden of the Heavenly Father's Will. The eyes and ears of the heart will become the means for which to understand.

All must work unceasingly for the conversion of sinners, for without conversion one cannot receive all that God wishes for you.

All my children must die to oneself, each day, in order to completely abandon oneself to our Lord and Savior, Jesus Christ.

Pray, pray, *pray*, that the Holy Spirit showers you with the graces of His gifts. Let Him lead you and direct you always.

It is a time of redemptive prayer and suffering, for you shall all be severely tested in all your endeavors. Those who have remained faithful have nothing to fear, for they shall remain under the protection of my motherly love.

My love and my prayers are for all who *wish* for them. *Ask* for my intercession, my children, for all your needs.

I will love you *always*, my dearest children. Go now in Peace, Love and Mercy, always."

APRIL 15, 1998

We were sick with a stomach virus and could not be in prayer on the 13th to receive her worldwide message.

Our heavenly mother said: "Oh, my dearest children of the world, I urge you to continuously pray for the conversion of lost souls and yourselves. For without conversion of heart, a soul cannot receive anything that God wishes for it. This process is a result of the Divine Love that our Heavenly Father has for each of His children.

A soul cannot find our Lord and Savior Jesus Christ when it is drowning in the illusions caused by Satan, or blinded by the false promises of a sensual world. The success of the world promises belongs to its endeavors.

Pray, pray, *pray*, my beloved ones, the most Holy Rosary daily, for *much* prayer is needed for the many sins committed in this world today. Carry your crosses each day, and lift up your sufferings in union with my Son, where you shall receive peace, joy and love in your lives, for many of my children do not realize the rewards for embracing their crosses.

My Son's Cross is a sign of the Love for each one of us. The future of the world is dependent upon love, my dearest ones.

Your faith and perseverance will be severely tested in these End Times, which will require every ounce of your strength. A child who remains spiritually blind can not see the many choices, but chooses only those which are pleasing to the senses.

Continue to receive the Body, Blood, Soul and Divinity of our Lord and Savior, Jesus Christ, in the most Holy Eucharist daily, to nourish and strengthen your souls. And in these last days of darkness, a light shall pour forth for the purification of the world. Believe and trust in me, your heavenly mother, that all will be purified and that a new-dawn day *will* come forth, a day in which love will flourish.

You shall soon see many wonders performed by our Heavenly Father. Your food supplies are diminishing, which shall lead to a world wide famine, and as darkness envelopes the world there shall be much chaos, bloodshed and natural disasters day after day. And when these events unfold, the evil head of the Anti-Christ shall surface.

A rumble shall soon be felt around the world which will cause much anguish. The darkness that will beseech the world is beyond description. My children must be spiritually and physically prepared in order to remain in harmony with me, your heavenly mother, through these End Times.

All that has been written in Scripture will be fulfilled, including the Second Coming of our Lord and Savior, Jesus Christ. The grain of wheat shall be your symbol for the events that will unfold.

There is much joy in Heaven in knowing the good that will come from this purification. You shall receive much humility, obedience, and love, and much shall be expected of you. Pray, that the eyes of the heart of my children who have remained closed, open and begin to listen and live all that I have been teaching.

Continue to praise and give thanks to our Heavenly Father, especially for the gift of life. And as we journey through these End Times, hold my hand.

I love you, my children. I will always love you my children. Continue to pray and remain obedient and trusting in our Lord and Savior, Jesus Christ."

MAY 13, 1998

Our heavenly mother said: "Oh, my dearest children of the world, pour yourselves out in praise, love and gratitude to our Lord and Savior Jesus Christ. And let my motherly spirit guide you in these times of action. Gratitude is the key to the heart of the Father. Each New Dawn morning should be seen as a renewed world, a new beginning in your preparation. Continue to follow the path and direction that our Heavenly Father wishes for you. Be content with the Divine Plan that He wishes for you. Only by saying 'yes' to the heavenly Divine invitation, will you ever accomplish anything in your lives. Bask in the light, the light that radiates from within the hearts of those who have remained faithful to me, your heavenly mother.

You are instruments of your own free will. To do the Will of Heaven is the greatest act of mercy that one can perform for the world. In these End Times in which you live, under the influence of the Evil One, who is at his highest strength, can only be defeated by the power of God.

Continue to work for the conversion of sinners. My Son is Love, Mercy, Peace and Forgiveness. I ask you, my dearest little ones, to act now in courage on behalf of my Son, our Lord and Savior, Jesus Christ. Trust in me, your heavenly mother, that I will protect and guide each of you. It is good to know that while you live on Earth, my Son has prepared a permanent home for you in Heaven.

There will be much suffering for those who have chosen the path of the Cross. Yet you will discover the joys that it will bring in your lives. I will clothe you in the finest garments and embellish you in all my motherly virtues. Those who have remained faithful will become One in union with the Sacred Heart of my Son, Jesus Christ and the Immaculate Heart of your heavenly mother. And as I am preparing you for a new life, I ask you to continually be obedient to the teachings of my Son's Church.

The Church is undergoing its greatest trial now. In this hour, I am in my final battle with Satan, and I assure you that my Immaculate Heart *shall* triumph, resulting in the most beautiful crown of glory.

Go now, my Children, and bask in the illumined joy of my love.

I love you, my dearest little ones, with all my motherly love. Hold on to my hands as I walk with you through these End Times and into the New Era of Peace.

I love you, my children. I *love* you, my children, I will *always* love you, my dearest little children!"

JUNE 13, 1998

Our heavenly mother said: "Oh, My beloved children, never in these present times has my heart trembled with my motherly love for those whom our Heavenly Father entrusted to me. You are living in a corrupted and unhealthy world caused by the snares of Satan, which is enabling you to respond to my urgent appeal.

I am the New-Dawn Day, bringing Light to the darkness, a Light which covers the poor, shelter where the greatest event in history is about to unfold upon the world.

You are being lost along the paths of sinfulness, in a world in which my adversary seems to reign. A message springs forth from my Immaculate Heart as a source of faith and comfort to all my faithful children.

Continuously pray for the graces of the Holy Spirit's gifts, for the direction and guidance in your lives.

Mortify yourself through penance, humility and fasting.

Please, my dearest children, desire me as much as I desire you. Consecrate continuously yourselves to my Immaculate Heart in order that you may live in daily communion of lives with our Lord and Savior, Jesus Christ. Pour out yourselves in grace, love and gratitude.

I am the gate which will open to the New Era of Peace. I am the Mother of the Second Advent, preparing my children for the glorious return of our Lord and Savior, Jesus Christ into the world in which he was born.

My motherly soul is pierced as my Son's Church prostrates beneath the weight of the agony of pain. My beloved Pope becomes more and more and more ridiculed, mocked, isolated and abandoned. Many bishops and priests have taken the road of unholiness. These wolves in sheep's clothing inflict slaughter upon the sheepfold of my Son, Jesus Christ.

My dearest little children, a great war is on the horizons. *Please*, my dearest children, pray, pray, pray the most holy Rosary to *avert* this war!

As a concerned mother, I am announcing that the events of these final times are about to happen to the world. Those who have been entrusted by our Heavenly Father to lead will be impeded by the evil of the world. My children who have remained faithful have nothing to fear, for they will remain protected under my mantle of Love.

Do *not* be frightened, for my Son, Jesus Christ, is always with you. With courage, spread throughout the world the Light of Love, the Light of Grace, the Light of Truth, and the Light of Holiness.

In this the final hour, I am asking all my children for prayers, suffering and total immolation of yourselves.

You must remain in a divine state of grace in order to receive our Lord and Savior, Jesus Christ.

I love you, my dearest children, I love you my dearest children, I will *always* love you, my dearest little children.

Please hold on to my hands as I walk with you into the New Era of Peace, Love, Joy and Holiness.

JULY 9, 1998

Our heavenly mother said: "My dearest children, why do you continuously *ignore* the many signs that are being given to you from our Father in Heaven? My motherly concern is great, because this generation is continuing in its obstinate rejection of God. In many ways I have intervened and urged you towards conversion of heart and soul and to return to my Son, our Lord and Savior Jesus Christ.

God is the Father and Creator of all people. The eyes of the heart remain closed for many of my children who are unable to see the light of truth. The faith of all my children must grow, to sustain, for the chastisements which await you. I urge you to do this *now*, to prepare yourselves for the New Era of Peace.

At Fatima, I have foretold to you when the True Faith would be lost. These are the times. And as my adversary deceives many, the darkness will grow deeper and deeper, and sin will cover everything, but you must clothe yourselves in divine grace.

Satan will seduce you by pride, doubt, unbelief and discouragement, resulting in much confusion. Avoid everything that disturbs the spirit and focus on the Cross, the sign of your salvation.

Pray, pray, *pray*, my children, for a World War is on the horizon! Much prayer is needed to prevent the bloodshed and loss of many lives. You shall see many unbelievable events and wonders worked by the hand of my Son, as the trials accompanying this time will be limitless. Even in my Son's Church, the crisis has become more acute as many of my beloved priests do not heed my voice. They scatter the flock along the roads of insecurity and division, of error and apostasy.

Yes, at this very moment, when my adversary is triumphing everywhere, my Immaculate Heart weeps in sorrow for the unfaithfulness of my children. And as the darkness envelops the world, the clearer will be the Light which shines forth from my Immaculate Heart that will show the Remnant the ways to follow.

Heed my warnings, my dear little children, and stay in the safe harbor of my Heart. Your hope, trust, and faith will be rewarded when the New Dawn day comes.

My love is yours, my children. It is all that you will ever need for complete protection and the fulfillment of your needs and desires.

Continue to remain at peace as you hold onto my motherly hand.

Go now in the happiness and Love of our Lord and Savior Jesus Christ."

JULY 13, 1998

Our heavenly mother said: "My dearest children of the world, I, your heavenly mother, am presenting myself in extraordinary ways in order to help you grow in love, unity, and to obtain the gifts of the Holy Spirit. Spread the light of Truth in these, the End Times, where darkness spreads everywhere. And even in the darkness and coldness, I urge you to live in hope and great trust.

My Son, our Lord and Savior Jesus Christ, is sending me to you to bring you His salvation. Praise Him and open up your hearts to receiving this gift with humility and gratitude. Spread everywhere the perfume of my presence and motherly love.

Visit often my Son in the Blessed Sacrament, in order to become refreshed and receive the peace and graces necessary to fulfilling your mission in life, according to the plan for each of you made by our Father in Heaven. Thank Him and praise Him for the gracious good on your behalf.

My Immaculate Heart is immersed in a sea of sorrow, for many of my children have not listened to my urgent calling for conversion and repentance.

I am the Queen of the Most Holy Rosary. Pray, pray, *pray* with me, my little ones, each day. **The Rosary will become your weapon against Satan in these End Times.**

I am the New-Dawn Spring, bringing graces to those who have remained faithful. In the garden of my Immaculate Heart, a Light shines, causing the most beautiful of flowers to spring up, The Light of Divine Grace; the Light of my Son, Jesus Christ.

The virtue of patience will become very important in your future. Strengthen yourselves by receiving the Body, Blood, Soul and Divinity of Our Lord and Savior Jesus Christ in the Most Holy Eucharist each day.

Many of my children *still* refuse to believe the signs that Our Father in Heaven is sending them. Trust and believe in me, your heavenly mother, that all is about to be purified, giving way to a New-Dawn Day, a New Era of Peace, and the glorious return of Our Lord and Savior Jesus Christ.

Do *not* allow yourselves to become seized in fear, doubt, discouragement and above all, confusion, caused by my adversary. Please, my dearest children, come to me and let me comfort you in the refuge of my arms.

The time has come for your sufferings to begin, as you witness the sins of your souls. I am the Virgin Mother, the New-Day Spring. Do not be frightened and seek refuge in my

Immaculate Heart.

I love you, my dearest little children, I love you my dearest little children, I will *always* love you my dearest little children.

Go now, and let our Father's Will be done."

AUGUST 13, 1998

Our heavenly mother said: "My dearest little ones of the world in the mantle of my Immaculate Heart, I offer you to the glory of the Most Holy Trinity.

Please have more patience for all to occur in your lives. I am revealing myself in extraordinary ways to show you the path to salvation.

Today, I am leading you into the Light, which will give you the strength to fight against the darkness of sin and the powers of evil. I am showing you the ways that you must follow. This is done, my children, with constant, vigilant prayers to our Lord and Savior, Jesus Christ, allowing for the conversion of the heart and soul in the divine Grace to change your lives to holiness.

Many signs are being given to you from Our Heavenly Father, calling for repentance and change of heart, for those who have a conversion of heart and soul will be needed to console those who are confused by my adversary. Yet, the eyes of the hearts of many of my children remain closed to these signs, and they live in the apostasy of hatred and sin.

The evil head of the Anti-Christ is about to surface and the final battle of souls has now come. I am the Immaculate Conception, preparing my children for the suffering and pains of purification.

These are the End Times. Time is running out; I can no longer hold back the hand of our Heavenly Father. Humanity has chosen an unhealthy road to follow in its rebellion against God.

Consecrate yourselves to me, your heavenly mother, each day, which will allow my motherly love and illuminating light to inflame your hearts and souls.

Please, my dear children, pray, Pray, *pray* the most Holy Rosary, for much prayer and fasting is needed, especially when adoring before the Blessed Sacrament! A deep trust and total unity with our Lord and Savior Jesus Christ is needed for the Spirit of Wisdom and Truth to prevail.

I am The Coredemptrix and Mediatrix of All Graces, preparing my children on the altar of My Immaculate Heart for the glorious return of our Lord and Savior, Jesus Christ. And when the light of my Immaculate Heart has transformed this sensual, meaningless world, my Son will descend in His glory to restore His Kingdom.

Please, my children, *heed* my warnings: a World War is developing and the evil face of my adversary is at work, which will cause much suffering and the loss of many lives. And when the New Dawn Day brings forth its light, bask in the Divine Love of our Lord and Savior Jesus Christ for your protection and guidance.

I love you my children, I love you my children, I love you my children....

Go now in Peace, unity, and everlasting Love."

SEPTEMBER 13, 1998

Our heavenly mother said, "My dearest children of the world, I am embracing you with the love from my Immaculate Heart as a sign of salvation. **The destruction which awaits you is beyond human description for many of my children still have not listened to my pleas.** They do not pray the most holy Rosary and continue to live the sinful ways in their lives which is menaced by my adversary. He has succeeded in spreading his deceitful ways into their lives.

In this era which is about to end, I have been successful in holding back the chastisements because of the prayers and sufferings from my remnant few. And as darkness grows deeper over the world, the Divine hand of justice shall descend for the purification through darkness, fire and blood. And as your souls are revealed to you, do not be frightened but remain under the mantle of my motherly protection.

Please, my dearest little children, pray to the Holy Spirit to receive His virtues for the strength, guidance and courage that you will need in these end times. My Son's light will continuously shine on each of you showing you the ways that you must follow.

The day and the hour have come upon the world. I am the mother to all, I am the way of peace, for it is through me that I am bringing you back to God. I am the New Dawn Spring arising to announce the bright light of our Lord and Savior, Jesus Christ.

My Son's church is at its greatest trial now where apostasy and error spread everywhere. Yet the divine light of truth shall triumph resulting in the resurrection of the renewed church through our Lord and Savior, Jesus Christ.

Pray, pray, pray my children, that you live within me, for this is the final hour.

The year shall not end without a great sign being given to mankind. And as the love and spirit of our Lord and Savior, Jesus Christ spreads everywhere, it shall transform the callous hearts and souls of many of my children. In order for you to fight my adversary you must call upon the Holy Spirit for strength and perseverance. The evil one has reached his highest power now, and your survival will depend upon your total abandonment to our Lord and Savior, Jesus Christ.

I am the mother of the church bringing salvation and hope to all of my children, and when you have become transfigured will the image of my Immaculate Heart and the Sacred Heart of our Lord and Savior, Jesus Christ be imposed upon your hearts and souls. Bask in the internal glory of our Father in Heaven where you shall live in his peace, love and kindness.

I love you my children, I love you my children, I will always love you my children. Go now and rejoice for the final hour has come upon the world. Amen."

Personal Messages

PERSONAL MESSAGES FROM OUR HEAVENLY MOTHER FROM SEPTEMBER, 1997

When our heavenly mother arrives on the 13th of each month, and occasionally on other days, she begins with personal messages. She has requested that these personal messages be included in her book.

Before our heavenly mother arrives, we always begin the most holy Rosary. We always bless her with holy water, while saying, "We Bless you O, heavenly mother, in the Name of the Father, the Son, and the Holy Spirit. If you are not of God be gone." She requested that we always do this.

SEPTEMBER 13, 1997

Our heavenly mother said: "As my chosen children, I shower you this day and every day with an abundance of my motherly love, and as I have said before, you, my daughter and son, are so very, very dear to my Immaculate Heart. I pour out an abundance of love to you both, and thank the Father each day for giving me to you as your mother in Heaven. And, as I have asked, we will now recite together that prayer which I have given to you, my daughter, to our Father in Heaven; and as we recite together that prayer from my heart to your heart, I will ask all the angels in Heaven, all the saints, St. Michael, and my Son, our Lord and Savior Jesus Christ, to recite this prayer with you to our Heavenly Father."

SEPTEMBER 20, 1997

Our heavenly mother said: "My chosen children, thank you for reciting that beautiful holy Rosary, which I, your heavenly mother, requested. I shower you tonight with my love, and bring with me my Son's love, our Lord and Savior, Jesus Christ. And yes, my daughter and son, a gift was bestowed upon you as chosen children. You will not only cherish that gift, but you will love that gift with all your heart, and with all your soul, for as I have foretold you, you will see and you will experience many things that many of my children will cherish, and, as your mother, I solemnly promise you that what I have foretold you will come to pass.

This night I descend upon you, my chosen daughter, to deliver to you what our Father in Heaven has graced you with, through me, your heavenly mother. And as we look back, your obedience, your faith and your trust has led you to your state of being, and now your final transformation has come. The prayers and the messages have made you grow physically to become much stronger in your faith, physically much stronger to bear and carry the crosses from my Son, and physically to bear persecutions that you will face. And you have grown mentally in understanding the Word of God the Father, his Son, our Lord and Savior, Jesus Christ, and me, your heavenly mother. And mentally you have been prepared as a chosen child to receive these special graces through our Father in Heaven, and you will continue to be graced to go forth with your mission in life. And you will be taught by my Son, Jesus Christ, and be filled with the Holy Spirit to go forward to proclaim the Good News of our Father in Heaven, and prepare for the final battle between good and evil."

OCTOBER 13, 1997

Our heavenly mother said: "My beloved daughter and son, it gives me, your heavenly mother, much joy in knowing the time I will spend with you, my chosen children. I look forward to this day in spending my time with you, the 'two hearts' brought together as one. Become embraced, my daughter and son, with the love that flows from my heart to your hearts, become embraced in my light, as I lift you up with me to Heaven. The time of which I, your heavenly mother, have spoken to you, my chosen children, has come. And as we spend this time together, open up your hearts and souls to me, your heavenly mother, and let the Holy Spirit fill your hearts and souls with His presence, and ponder what I will tell you this evening.

Always remember that you, my daughter and son, are very, very special to me, your heavenly mother. And, as I gaze down upon you, I see the trials and persecutions that you are undergoing. But I am always with you, with my Son, our Lord and Savior, Jesus Christ, to give you the strength to endure the trials and persecutions, but most importantly, to fill your hearts and souls with Our Love from my Immaculate Heart and the Sacred Heart of my Son, in which you shall love others in return.

Oh, my dear little children, you make my heart leap with joy, and as I look down upon you, I grace you with my motherly love. Remember, my daughter and son, that what I am telling you, my children will never understand, for you have been chosen by our Father in Heaven. And yes, my beloved daughter, my Son sends His Love to you, and He waits for the day in which you shall enter Paradise with Him.

I come to you both in sadness, for sins continue to make the cup overflow, and the time has come for which we have spoken about. We will continue to pray the Rosary, and when we pray we will pray the Sorrowful Mysteries, for tonight, what I, your heavenly mother, bring to you, my beloved children, will bring much pain to my children. But always remember that the Sorrowful Mysteries end in the salvation of your souls. And, as we say the Sorrowful Mysteries, think of the suffering of my Son, our Lord and Savior, Jesus Christ, in knowing that He had suffered for us, for our sins. And now, my beloved daughter and son, my children will suffer for *their* sins.

And now, let us begin the Sorrowful Mysteries with the Agony in the Garden. In the name of the Father, the Son and the Holy Spirit. Amen...."

NOVEMBER 13, 1997

Our heavenly mother said: "My beloved daughter and son, it gives me much joy and love to be present here tonight with you, my chosen children. And as I grace you with my love and presence, open up your hearts and souls to receive my love. And let my beloved Spouse, the Holy Spirit, enter into you. For tonight, my chosen children, you must discern what I foretell you, for the *time is short* for the Holy Spirit to guide you and give you the discernment to understand what is needed to decipher what is of God and what is of my Adversary.

We will pray the Sorrowful Mysteries, for as I have foretold you, you will suffer for my Son, our Lord and Savior, Jesus Christ, as he has suffered for you, for our sins. And as we say the Sorrowful Mysteries, embrace them with your love, in knowing that your salvation is at hand. And comfort yourself, with the blood that He shed for you, and quench your thirst. And so let us begin, my daughter and son. In the name of the Father, the Son and the Holy Spirit. Amen.

My beloved daughter and son, open up your hands, and repeat after me:

O, Holy Spirit, my beloved Spouse,
I call upon you to descend to my chosen children
and kindle within their hearts and souls your presence,
so that they may come to understand what I am about to
foretell them. And give them the strength to endure the
trials and persecutions which they are about to undergo.

My beloved daughter and son, the End Times have now come upon us, and as I have prepared you, you must now prepare my children. And you shall see the unfolding of events, which shall take place in rapid succession. The evil head of the Anti-Christ will now rise in conjunction with the Anti-Pope. My Son's Church prostrates, caused by the schisms within the Church, which is causing the division of the Catholic religion, and soon your daily Mass will be held underground, as the cohorts of the Anti-Christ seek to destroy those who follow my Son, our Lord and Savior, Jesus Christ. Prepare your souls, for the final battle is about to begin.

Always remember what I have taught you, that your salvation will come through my Son, and your glory is given through the grace of our Father in Heaven. And blessed are you, my chosen children, for you have been given much, and you will see a new Earth with beauty unknown to mankind. And even throughout your lives, my daughter and son, the greatest joy that you ever experienced can not compare for what you are about to be given. And, yes, you are highly favored by our Father in Heaven. And blessed are you, my daughter and son, for accepting the invitation for our Father's Will be done. And your journey will now begin, as I bring my children to you, you shall teach them and you shall show them what I have given you. Always remember to call on the Holy Spirit to guide you and let His words speak through you. Speak with authority and do not fear, for I will always be there to protect you."

DECEMBER 13, 1997

Our heavenly mother said: "My beloved daughter and son, I come before you tonight with a heavy heart for the sins in the world, for many of my children continue to live in darkness. For what I have foretold you will now come to being, and as the events unfold, you shall bear witness for what I have foretold you.

We now live in the End Times. You must continue to pray and follow your journey for which I have foretold you. The time is short and the harvest is great, but the workers are few.

My beloved chosen children, I grace you tonight with my motherly love. As we prepare for the final battle, you must always remember what I have taught you, so that you may teach others. For everything must be stored within your soul. *Prepare*, my dear little children."

JANUARY 5, 1998

Our heavenly mother said: "My beloved daughter and son, my heart leaps with joy in coming at your beck and call. Blessed are you, my chosen children, my 'two hearts' as one, my gift from our Father in Heaven. It pleases me to see my two chosen hearts pay reverence to our Lord and Savior, Jesus Christ, our Savior, our Shepherd. Your souls leap with joy as my Spouse lives within you through the graces of our Father in Heaven. And why, my children, do you call me to your presence this evening?

My beloved daughter and son, your journey takes you in many directions. As your heavenly mother, I am proud in knowing that my 'two hearts as one' spread the Word of God amongst my children. I send forth my love to you both, for as my children, I am proud of you as your mother. And while in your presence this evening I would like you to join me in prayer, and we shall say together the Joyful Mysteries, as Christmas comes to a close today, for the journey of the wise men has ended in the offering of gifts to my beloved Son. And tonight, my beloved daughter and son, you shall pour forth your gifts of love unto Him, and together, with me, we shall pray from our hearts and souls.

As the wise men came bearing gifts of gold, your prayers tonight are much finer than gold, whose fragrance ascends unto Heaven to my Son, our Lord and Savior, Jesus Christ. And remember, my beloved daughter and son, the birth of our Savior is a birth of *all* of us into the Kingdom of Heaven, the *true* meaning of Christmas.

My beloved daughter and son, your souls are cleansed, reap the graces that pour forth from our Heavenly Father unto your souls and rejoice in knowing that you are highly favored by our Father. And as your bodies burn with the Holy Spirit, it kindles the light of love that you have for my Son, our Lord and Savior, Jesus Christ, and as your love becomes stronger, so too shall the flame, for you have now become a holy temple for his Sacred Heart and the heart of your heavenly mother.

And so you are blessed, and so you are favored, and so you shall journey in doing the work of our Father in Heaven, for the time is short, and many of my children are lost.

Let us now pray the Joyful Mysteries...."

JANUARY 13, 1998

Our heavenly mother said: "My beloved chosen children, it pleases me, your heavenly mother, to come to you with the graces of our Heavenly Father. I pour forth my love to you.

Your presence and love fills me with much joy in knowing the reverence you pay to my Son, our Lord and Savior, Jesus Christ.

The gifts given to you by our Heavenly Father are tools for you to use to bear the fruits in carrying out the heavenly Divine plan. All that I have foretold you is beginning to happen, yet my children *still* do not heed the warning given to them by Heaven!

The worldly events that you are witnessing will increase, as the time is short. O, my dear little children, you will be my instruments, my Son's instruments, in fighting the spiritual battle to save souls. Your persecutions and trials will increase many-fold, but understand that you are under the mantle of my protection, for I hold you close to my Immaculate Heart and my Son holds you close to his Sacred Heart.

Through the Sacrament of Reconciliation, remain pure as a temple for the Sacred Heart and the Immaculate Heart that will reign within your soul.

Let us pray the Glorious Mysteries together, and as we say them, let our prayers be lifted into Heaven. And remember, my dear little children, the souls in Purgatory, for your prayers are needed, as they seek the Kingdom of my Son, Paradise, and a fulfillment of the Divine Will of God, our Heavenly Father."

FEBRUARY 13, 1998

Our heavenly mother said: "My dear, dear little children, I send forth to you my motherly love. Let us pray the last Hail Mary to complete the decade for which you had begun.'

As you hold tightly the cross which bears the crucifixion of my Son to your hearts, so too, do I hold you, my dear little children, to *my* heart, my 'two little hearts as one.'

Tonight, my dear children, I come to you in urgency in knowing that the time has come for which I have foretold you. You must prepare yourselves for the serious times that are about to begin. Always remember what I have taught you. Always focus on the Cross and always have my Son, our Lord and Savior, Jesus Christ, become the *center* of your life. And as you go forth in your journey to proclaim the word of our Father in Heaven, remember the persecutions and trials for which I have foretold you. And even as I speak to you this evening, my children still do not recognize my Son as their Lord and Savior, and the Creator, our Father in Heaven. And the signs of Heaven shall be intensified and you shall know that these are from God.

Brace yourselves, my children, for the cataclysmic events that you shall soon witness. And be prepared to follow your Angels to where they direct you to go, in the Name of our Lord and Savior, Jesus Christ.

My time with you, my children, will soon come to a close, but always remember I am a prayer away and will hold you close to my Immaculate Heart, where you shall hold me close to your heart with my Son, Jesus Christ.

Your faith shall be tested, my dearest little children. You have served the Shepherd well. You live a life according to the Will of our Father in Heaven, for that is why your life is filled with love, peace and joy. Let us together say the Glorious Mysteries this evening. It gives me much joy and pleasure in saying the holy Rosary with my two hearts as one, for you fill my heart with joy and your love. And as I pour forth my love unto you, open your hearts and souls to receive this precious gift from our Father in Heaven and let it flow like a river flows into the ocean. For your soul has no depth or width and is infinite just as eternity is infinite. Let us begin...."

FEBRUARY 16, 1998

Our heavenly mother appeared around 9:15 p.m. She was dressed in a white dress with a powder-blue veil. She had crystal Rosary beads in her hands. She delivered the following message for us, her chosen children.

Our heavenly mother said: "The time for which I speak will be short, but will be very devastating. This will be a time of great grace and Mercy for all my faithful children. Be prepared *now*, my chosen children, so you can help others when this time comes. Many will be lost because they will not serve.

The time has come for 'Thy Kingdom come.' It will be your love that brings you to a new-dawn day, to a continued faith and understanding. You will be busy at all hours of the day and night proclaiming the word of our Father in Heaven.

In preparation for the time when you will no longer see me, praise and pay reverence to our Lord and Savior Jesus Christ, to erase the great doubt that will enter into your hearts.

My Son's flesh is given for *all*, for the life of the world. The prayers I have given you will work miracles in the lives and hearts of the lost, lonely children. All my children will live in danger and fear, and think only how to survive the times of evil. It will be a time of much confusion as my dearest little children seek the truth and ways to turn. My faithful will have nothing to fear, for their protection will be within my mantle.

Pray, pray, *pray* the Rosary. Meditate on the Mysteries each day, for vigils of prayer are most important. I am the Day Spring, bringing life to my children who have remained spiritually blind and do not see with the eyes of their hearts and souls.

So do not worry, my little ones, for what the future holds, for *today* is what is important, and not tomorrow. Your sanctity is what is at risk. All is in the final process of purification and my children are to listen most attentively to my Beloved Spouse, the Holy Spirit, who with me, your heavenly mother, will instruct and guide each of you. We will then be as one, think as one, love as one, trust as one and praise and glorify the Almighty One, our Father in Heaven, as one.

You must *not* give in to the Evil One's deception, who will try to lead you away from my Son, Jesus Christ. The forces of evil will not stop until they are completely destroyed by God at the appointed time.

Continue to receive the Body, Blood, Soul and Divinity of my Son, Jesus Christ, in the most Holy Eucharist.

I love you, my dearest chosen children!

Go in peace for now, and please continue to hold my hand, my dear ones."

FEBRUARY 17, 1998

Our heavenly mother said: "O, my dear, dear, little children; as your heavenly mother, I have promised to be with you in your journey. I come to you in your needs as you prepare for this special journey. I, your heavenly mother, shall be with you always. *Trust* in me and my Son, Jesus Christ.

O, My sweet, sweet daughter and son, your fragrance of love fills my Immaculate Heart this evening; you bring me much joy in knowing the reverence you pay my Son each day. The obedience and perseverance in your faith leads you down the road of holiness. Continue to remain faithful, continue to trust, and remain focused on the Cross, your salvation and tool of redemption.

As a seedling thirsts for water at the height of the day, so too do you, my daughter and son, thirst for the Love of my Son. It is this Love that nourishes you both, it is this Love that gives you the peace, the joy, and the happiness. It is this Love that makes my 'two hearts as one' beat as one, in union with me your heavenly mother and the Sacred Heart of my Son, Jesus Christ, to our Father in Heaven. Each morning you rise to a new day, you bring joy to me for which you have spoken.

Your thirst is quenched not by the materialistic things of a sensual world, but the gold of the *real* world, gold that has come refined within your hearts that makes you radiate the Love of my Son, Jesus Christ, from your souls.

You, my daughter and son, live *life*, while many of my children do not. They merely 'exist.' It is sad for me, your heavenly mother, to see many of my children live in darkness. Please, my chosen children, go forth and *show* them the light!

The time is short, for which I speak. The energy that you are given through the Holy Spirit will continue to endure and strengthen you to go forth to proclaim the Word of our Father in Heaven.

It is your faith, as you have mentioned, that allows you to receive my Son. Your trust and your faith allows you to receive the Eucharist to nourish your soul and your heart, and it is this faith that will continue to sustain you in the End Times.

You have shown our Father in Heaven that many of my children lack faith in their Creator, the Almighty One. Your faith represents an abundance of reverence for Him, your Creator. Continue as you have, my little daughter and son, and your rewards will be bountiful. And always remember that no matter how difficult the tasks may seem, always trust and have faith in my Son, Jesus Christ, to prevail. The truth will prevail always over evil. And when confusion prevents you to see the Light, call upon me, your heavenly mother, to lead you and show you the way. Now let us say the Joyful Mysteries of the Most Holy Rosary...."

MARCH 10, 1998

Our heavenly mother said: "My dearest little children, during this Lenten season, pay reverence to my Son, our Lord and Savior, Jesus Christ, through penance and fasting. Become united as one with Him through the forgiveness of sins and His Mercy, which has no boundaries. My dearest daughter, your hearts leap with joy, for the presence of my Son flows within you; His Divine Love fills your hearts and souls, for the time for which I have spoken has come upon the world and you shall see the wonders for which I have foretold you.

Satan will try to discourage you in the faith that you must place in my Son, Jesus Christ in these End Times. Your consecration and my Son's Mercy is what is needed to sustain you in these times. Our Lord and Savior Jesus Christ's presence becomes manifested in those faithful souls of my chosen children, as we prepare for His crucifixion on Mount Calvary. And now, my 'two hearts as one,' on that day you shall feel the pains of suffering.

As your heavenly mother, I ask you to fast until the death of my Son and on that day, you shall pray for which I shall speak on the 13th for this preparation, and on that day you shall experience what I, your heavenly mother, have experienced, and you shall come to know your Lord crowned with thorns.

You shall come to know the sins of the world, which He carried on His shoulder and you shall come to know the salvation of your souls, and together we shall mourn, and together we shall rejoice, for a new-dawn day has come upon us. Let the Holy Spirit flow into you to guide you and teach you.

O, my dearest chosen children, you are to go forth and bring to my Son, our Lord and Savior, Jesus Christ, the sinners of the world and you shall deliver them to Him.

My beloved Spouse, the Holy Spirit, enters into you now to prepare you for this Lenten season, to prepare you and strengthen you for His crucifixion so that you may have the strength to endure the pains which will become a part of you, and you shall lift up those pains with your Lord and Savior for all sinners of the world.

My dearest daughter and son, your hearts beat for the love of your Lord and Savior, the Light that gives Life to you now, the Peace that surrounds the life, and as I speak to you, feel your souls being lifted into Heaven as your bodies become light, as they are lifted within my mantle and carried into Heaven.

Feel the Love that is beginning to surround you. It is this Love for which you seek, it is this Love that awaits you at the end of your life's journey for which my Son has prepared a place for you, my 'two hearts as one.' And, as you begin to experience the presence of Heaven, you are beginning to witness all the things for which I have foretold you which many of my children would cherish to see. For you see and hear with your eyes and ears of the heart; it is here that the truth lives. For the eyes and the ears of the heart cannot be deceived by the Evil One; it is here that you will hold your Lord and Savior.

My Son pours forth His Divine Love unto you, continue to remain obedient and humble yourself always in reverence to Him, your Savior, for it is through Him an eternal life exists. It is through Him that death has no claim on a faithful soul, it is through Him that shines forth the light.

Continue to Pray, Pray, ***Pray***, my dearest daughter and son, for your prayers are jewels which adorn my crown. And as I look down upon you my two 'little hearts as one,' I pour forth my motherly love unto you, my chosen children.

Continue to follow me, for I am pleased that you listen to my words which many of my children ignore, for the day is coming, the Day of the Lord."

MARCH 13, 1998

Our heavenly mother said: "My beloved chosen children, just as these roses that you placed before me bring the sweet fragrance to you, so do you bring a sweet fragrance to me in your presence. You, my daughter and son, are so precious to me, my 'two hearts as one,' given to me as a gift from our Heavenly Father. In this special evening you will ponder in your hearts all that I am about to tell you.

As I look before me, I see the journey, that all your family will go out into the desert. And as the Jews exited Egypt, so too now, you shall exit this world, which will be controlled by Satan. And you shall go forth into the desert and you shall find the Promised Land, the land of milk and honey. And when you have found the Promised Land, there you shall find my Son, our Lord and Savior Jesus Christ, waiting for you.

And in your journey, you shall encounter the forces of evil that will try to discourage you in your pursuit of happiness and peace. Always remain focused on the cross, your salvation, your redemption. And no matter how heavy that cross may be, always remember the Cross that my Son carried for you. And even as I speak these very words, His Love is being poured forth into your hearts, which are beginning to leap with love. Feel His presence within you, feel His Love for you, an unconditional Love, a Divine Love.

And now let us say the holy Rosary. As your heavenly mother, I am proud to hear that this Rosary will be given to the souls in Purgatory. We will pray the Sorrowful Mysteries in this, the Lenten season, in preparation for my Son's crucifixion. Let us begin to pray...."

APRIL 9, 1998

Our heavenly mother said: "My beloved children, my heart leaps with joy in your presence as we prepare for the crucifixion of our Lord and Savior, Jesus Christ. My Son's glory comes to being with the Father in Heaven, for his journey on earth comes to an end in the fulfillment of His Resurrection into his Kingdom, a promise to all who remain faithful to Him. And through His suffering, we are allowed to have everlasting life in His Kingdom, an eternity of love, peace, joy, and happiness.

If only my children would *listen* to me, their heavenly mother, the rewards for them would be bountiful. And as Heaven prepares for His crucifixion, I have come tonight to prepare you, my little daughter and son. And as a mother, I have watched over you, and you have done what is right in your heart and your soul. Your fasting, your prayers, and your love for my Son, have been lifted to Heaven. He sends His Love to you and pours forth His graces to your souls and your hearts.

I ask as your mother this evening, to open up your souls and hearts as we prepare for His crucifixion and Resurrection. In three dawn-days, you shall come into your glory as he has come into His glory. And as you receive Him, you shall feel a presence overcome you, the True Presence of His Body, Blood, Soul and Divinity in union with our Father in Heaven. It is at this hour that he entered into the Garden of Olives to pray to His Father in Heaven, 'Our Father, do not abandon me for the Hour has come, and let Thy will be done.' An echo, a reassurance of words for which I, your heavenly mother, have spoken. And so too, you, my dear little children, have spoken to our Father in Heaven, in proclaiming, '... let Thy Will be done to us.'

As we pray together the Sorrowful Mysteries, consecrate this hour for my Son in what He had to endure, the sufferings and pains for us. A Love so great that He accepted His crucifixion for the Love of His people. And yet today this world lives in darkness. It has forgotten the Love that my Son shed for all on the Cross.

But I assure you, my dear little children, as quoted in Scripture by our Heavenly Father, and soon to come to being, 'every knee shall bend' in the presence of our Lord and Savior, Jesus Christ.

My heart is filled with much sorrow, for my children live in a world of confusion, confusion caused through their own free will. In three dawn-days, I shall talk to you, my chosen children, about your journey which you are to embark upon. For the time is short, and your journey will be long.

Do *not* worry, or become frightened for, I, your heavenly mother, will protect you with my Mantle of Love. Always remember to focus on the Cross, your strength, your salvation.

Now, as we begin the Sorrowful Mysteries, open up your hearts and soul and join them with my Son in the Garden, as He prayed to our Father in Heaven. Suffer with Him at the pillar, endure the pains of thorns, feel the heaviness of the sins on your shoulders as you help carry His Cross to His death. And tomorrow you shall prepare.

Let us begin. In the name of the Father, the Son and the Holy Spirit. Amen...."

APRIL 15, 1998

We were sick with a stomach virus and could not be in prayer on the 13th to receive her worldwide message. During prayer of the Divine Mercy Chaplet, our heavenly mother appeared to us during the last decade.

Our heavenly mother said: "My dearest little children, it pleases me to see that you are both feeling much better this evening. I, your heavenly mother, send forth my motherly love and tenderness into your hearts and souls. Feel my warmth, bathe in my warmth and feel the comfort of my motherly love. I bring you tonight close to me and give you strength to continue on your journey.

We all rejoice in the glory of the Resurrection of our Lord and Savior, Jesus Christ. It is this gift through our Heavenly Father that is promised to all who believe and have faith and trust. It is through the Resurrection that eternal Life is granted; it is through the Resurrection that a new Life is born; it is through the Resurrection that the soul comes home to a place prepared by Our Heavenly Father,-- into a Kingdom where eternal love, happiness, peace, and joy, are everlasting. But my heart is saddened in seeing many of my children *still* not listening to my words, a world which is being enveloped into darkness by my Adversary, a world in which the simple pleasures assimilate the senses of my children.

As I have foretold you, the natural disasters which you are witnessing will increase in number, day after day after day, and they shall come to know that these are events from our Father in Heaven.

You, my dear little children, will soon go forth to proclaim all of what I have taught you and you shall preach the Word of God to all my children. Remain strong in faith, trust and obedience.

Your perseverance will be severely tested in these End Times, but always remember to focus on the Cross for your strength and remember that the Cross is the sign of your salvation, and love.

Soon, my dear little children, the love that you feel for each other will be felt by all, as my Son descends upon the world. And as I speak to you, let my beloved Spouse, the Holy Spirit, now descend upon you. And you shall feel His warmth enter into your hearts and soul.

Open your hearts and soul to the divine presence of our Heavenly Father, for it is through Him that all things are made possible. My Heart and my Son's Heart leap with joy in seeing you pray the three Mysteries which I have taught you. For *much* prayer is needed for the many sins being committed in the world today.

Continue to pray as you have, and be an example for many of my children who shall soon come to you in vast numbers, seeking the Light in which you bask in, which radiates from your souls and hearts unto them. They shall know you by this Light. You shall open up your arms and welcome them as brothers and sisters. You shall teach them, you shall show them, and you shall guide them to Our Lord and Savior, Jesus Christ. For the Holy Spirit that lives within you will guide you on what to say, when to say it, where to say it, and how to say it.

And you, my beloved daughter, I, your heavenly mother, am very proud of you for the strength in which you show your obedience, faith, and perseverance. This will lead you to many graces soon. The strength which you show is an example for all my children to see and bear witness to in these End Times.

Many things you will never understand, but remember, that there *is* a God, our Creator, Whose Divine Plan leads *all* on a journey. And in our journey, many things we can not comprehend, but must continue to accept and remain faithful and strong as you have, my dearest daughter.

Continue in your perseverance, remain strong, hold my hand tightly, as Satan attacks you and my Son even stronger in these End Times. And always remember he is the master of deceit, deceiving you in your mind, and unless the soul controls the mind, the mind will control the body.

And you, my son, will also be severely tested in these, the End Times. You too, shall remain strong and faithful, and even though you see, there are times that you do not believe.

Remember the apostles. In spending two years with my Son, Jesus Christ, Who walked the earth, they've seen many miracles performed by Him, they were witness to all, even his teachings, but yet at the end *they* did not believe.

Trust and faith are the two most important virtues. Remember them and ponder them in your hearts.

Let us pray together the Glorious Mysteries and let us rejoice in the resurrection, in the life to come. Your hearts and souls must radiate of the Love of our Lord as He came into His glory, and let us together come into *our* glory as we pray tonight.

Continue, my children, to nourish your souls, and always remember that my Son and me, your heavenly mother, will *always* love you. And one day you shall join us in Paradise, and together we shall be one family with our

Father in Heaven. In the name of the Father, the Son and the Holy Spirit. Amen...."

MAY 4, 1998

Joseph was alone in prayer during this apparition.

Our heavenly mother said: "My dearest son, continue to remain on the path of divine virtues. Keep the Holy Spirit close to your heart, and witness the abundance of fruits you shall yield.

My dearest one, when my children are consecrated to my Immaculate Heart, they should fear nothing in doing the work for our Lord and Savior Jesus Christ. My Adversary *cannot* touch those whom have given themselves to me of their own free will, for through my Heart, many doors will open leading to the Kingdom of my Son.

The Holy Spirit will continue to speak to those souls which remain open, and not closed. Carefully heed what He tells you. Meditate often, and slowly absorb what He is asking of you.

Pray, pray, ***pray intensely***, my son, because my Adversary is deceiving many and causing division within my Son's Church. The trials which will accompany this time will be limitless.

I am always with you, my son, and my loving little children. My presence will continually transform you and give you the strength to do the work of our Heavenly Father. For without prayers in your lives, peace will never exist!

My son, humility, obedience, and trust will become your biggest ally in these coming days. Humility is the humblest of hearts for all things.

The Next Dawn Day is crucial for the salvation of many souls. Please help me, my son, so together we can teach others how to live victorious lives in union with my Son, Jesus Christ. You will know your gifts, as you have come to know your heavenly mother.

Abandon yourselves, my children, from the pleasures of a sensual world, in order to seek the direction you must travel. My Son's path is the path of Light, which shall give sight to the spiritual blindness which is preventing the eyes of the heart to see. Without this, you will never find the truth.

You need to trust totally in me, your heavenly mother, to defend and protect you. Continue to have faith and trust in my words, for the times which you are living is for the salvation of the world.

Great will be the bloodshed and the terror of my poor little children. I will continue to shower you with my peace and necessary graces, in order for you to fulfill your mission according to the Divine Plan of the Heavenly Father.

Go now in the peace and love of my motherly presence.

I love you my son, I love you my son, I love you my son."

MAY 9, 1998

Our heavenly mother came to us during prayer of the most holy Rosary. For Mother's Day, we had placed two red roses in front of the statue of Our Blessed Mother.

"We love you O, heavenly mother, and thank you for joining us in prayer. We bless you O, heavenly mother, in the Name of the Father, the Son and the Holy Spirit. If you are not of God, be gone."

"We love you very much, and both of us, your children, cannot let this evening go by without wishing you, our heavenly mother, the Mother of our Lord and Savior, the mother of all of us, your children, a very special, blessed Mother's Day. We would like you, O, heavenly mother, to join us in this most holy Rosary, and this Rosary we lift up to you, our heavenly mother, for Mother's Day. We love you so very, very much."

Our heavenly mother said: "My beloved daughter and son, I am The Mother Of All Graces, for all of my children of the world. Thank you for this rose that you placed before me, it touches me deeply, but more so for the love that you have for me, your heavenly mother, and my Son, our Lord and Savior, Jesus Christ.

A flower withers in time, but your love does not, but has become stronger, and must remain strong to withstand the tests of time that you are undergoing, my 'two hearts as one.' Continue to follow your strength, and on this special day, honor me, your heavenly mother, by saying the Rosary as you have, for this is the greatest honor for me, your heavenly mother. For it serves as the greatest weapon against my Adversary, and also for the sins of the world.

Pray, pray, pray the Rosary, my dear little daughter and son! Your journey has now begun and soon you will be brought in many directions proclaiming the Word of God. You will now serve as you wish and pray for. Continue to remain obedient, faithful and trusting and embrace your crosses each day."

MAY 12, 1998

Our heavenly mother said: "O, My 'two little hearts as one,' your hearts are saddened, but yet you fail to heed what I, your heavenly mother, have foretold you.

You, my dearest daughter and son, say that you trust me, your heavenly mother, but yet your faith was lacking, for as I have said I would take care of your family.

And you, my son, you have disappointed me, your heavenly mother. I have asked you to remain strong. But yet, you remain weak, and my Adversary relentlessly attacks you, you fall victim to his deceitful ways. I have asked you to embrace the Cross, but yet you continually let go. His attacks will become greater and greater in time, as your journey has begun. You must remain strong as my daughter has, for a weak heart *cannot* sustain the attacks of my Adversary. Both hearts must remain strong as one heart in union with our Lord and Savior, Jesus Christ, for if one heart becomes weak, the other cannot sustain the strength to fight the battle alone.

Through the intercession of St. Theresa, I come to you tonight. She has seen the hurt, the confusion, caused by my Adversary. He laughs at you both, in knowing that you do not represent me, your heavenly mother, well.

I know, my 'two hearts as one,' that you love me with all your love, with all your strength and with all your soul, as you do my Son. But please, my dear little children, you must remain strong in these difficult times that you are facing. You know your weaknesses, concentrate on them and make them your strengths. Work on them with my beloved Spouse, the Holy Spirit, who will teach you of what to do and how to do it. When your heart remains closed, when you are in anger or confusion, my beloved

Spouse is unable to help you because you shut out Heaven and became part of a meaningless world which my Adversary thinks he controls, but soon my Immaculate Heart shall triumph. But I need you, my dear little children, to help me fight this battle. You must remain strong.

I come to you tonight as a concerned mother, for I see you wither, I see you fall victim to his deceitful ways. A gallant soldier stands his ground in the heat of battle, he fights with all his strength for his honor and for the glory of his leader. I, my children, am asking you to help fight the Battle with me.

Let us now say the most holy Rosary, our weapon against Satan, and when we pray the Rosary open up your hearts to receive the strength of the Holy Spirit, a gift from our Father in Heaven.

Close your eyes, and feel the warmth of the Spirit entering into your souls and your hearts, and feel the Love of my Son, our Lord and Savior, Jesus Christ."

MAY 13, 1998

Our heavenly mother said: "O, my little daughter and son, this evening is a special day, a special day in my life. It was on this day in 1917 that I made my first appearance in Fatima. My heart is saddened as I look upon the world and see my children drowning in their sins and wishing to follow the illusions and deceptions of my Adversary! The world in which you live, my little children, is becoming darkened, and as the light begins to fade. So too, is the love that the world has for my Son, our Lord and Savior, Jesus Christ.

The Third Secret that has been foretold in Fatima is about to unfold upon this world, a world which exists in the absence of God, one where coldness, sadness, jealously and hatred flourish. But yet, my remnant few continue to pray for the sins committed and ask for the intercession of Heaven.

Soon the hand of the Father shall fall, and every knee shall bend and you shall pay reverence to our Creator and you shall know that there is but *one* God, and that all things come *from* God, *through* God, and all things are made *possible* by God. And as I have foretold you, the natural disasters shall increase tenfold. Pestilence shall be worldwide.

You must remain strong, and have faith and trust, for faith is trust in the Will of God.

I hold my children's hands in these, the End Times, but yet many have fallen and become consumed in the sensual pleasures of a meaningless world, a world which soon will change, where the true essence of life shall breathe.

I am Coredemptrix and Mediatrix Of All Graces, intermediary of my Son, our Lord and Savior, Jesus Christ and Heaven. And for 81 years, the world still rejects my words spoken at Fatima.

Let us now pray the Glorious Mysteries on the most holy Rosary, and as we pray, we together, my children, shall lift up our prayers for the souls in Purgatory and for the sinners of the world."

JUNE 2, 1998

During the Joyful Mysteries, our heavenly mother arrived during the Second Decade. We bless you O, heavenly mother in the Name of the Father, the Son and the Holy Spirit. If you are not of God be gone....

Our heavenly mother said: "Within your hands you not only hold the salvation of your soul, but that of mankind in the crucifix, on which my Son was crucified for your sins. And as you hold onto this, let your heart and soul be filled with His love, the love that he poured forth for all of us.

It pleases me, my 'two hearts as one,' to see that you are obedient in praying for the souls in Purgatory, for as I have said, much prayer is needed! Continue to pray for these souls, continue to pray for the sins of the world, continue to work for the conversion of lost souls.

As we live in these End Times, my Adversary deceives many of my children who wander in darkness, who have become totally immersed in the sensual pleasures. Many have fallen away from the Faith.

Please, my dear little daughter and son, pray, pray, pray hard, for much prayer is needed in these End Times. Feel my motherly love as it is being poured out to you both. Feel my warmth, as I embrace you in my arms.

It pleases me to see the reverence that you pay my Son, our Lord and Savior, Jesus Christ. Even I remain obedient and kneel before our King. Many have taken Him for granted. Many do not recognize the True Presence of my Son in the Holy Eucharist.

I have come this evening to pray with you. Let us continue to pray the Joyful Mysteries, and I ask you, my little daughter, to lead us in these Mysteries, since they have found a special place in your heart, just as you, my daughter and son, have found a special place in my heart, and I in your heart. Everything that I say you know is true, for you feel with your hearts and souls.

I ask you, as your heavenly mother, to continue to remain obedient. Do not stray, remain focused, and remember what I have foretold you. I always look down upon you as your mother. You must continue to remain obedient.

Let us now complete the Joyful Mysteries, and it pleases me, your heavenly mother, to know that you, my little daughter, will lead us in these Mysteries; and it also pleases me to see that my 'two hearts as one' have remained obedient for what I have asked.

Think with your hearts, and not your minds, and there you shall feel my love, my Son's Love, His peace. And remember His gift that has been given to you can easily be taken away. Let us now begin...."

JUNE 13, 1998

My dearest little children, bless yourselves: In the Name of the Father, Son and Holy Spirit, Amen.

I, your heavenly mother, come to you tonight in *urgency* for the events that are about to unfold upon the world. My heart is saddened and heavy, in seeing the many offenses being committed against my Son, our Lord and Savior Jesus Christ: the abomination of the Holy Eucharist, the division in my Son's Church, the ridicule of my beloved Pope, the unholy paths my beloved bishops and priests follow.

Why, my 'two hearts as one,' have not my children heeded our Heavenly Father's warnings? Why have my children *not* responded to my appeal?

The time has come **in which our Heavenly Father will now lower his hand out of Love for all his peoples. Those who have remained faithful, the Remnant few, have nothing to fear and will remain within my mantle of protection.**

The natural disasters that you are witnessing will be increased in intensity and numbers. know, my children, that these are warnings of Heaven, warnings against the sins that are being committed in a corrupted world.

Yes, my little daughter, hold on tightly to each other, to one another. My Adversary thinks he reigns with power, and controls this meaningless world that many of my children have fallen victim to. Remember, it is the Sacred Heart of my Son, our Lord and Savior Jesus Christ, and the Immaculate Heart of your heavenly mother that will triumph at the end. And Satan will be chained in Hell, and the New Era of Peace shall rein.

Prepare my dear little children, prepare, prepare, for what is to come, for what I have foretold you!

Continue to pray the most holy Rosary, continue to attend daily Mass, continue to receive the Body, Blood, Soul and Divinity of our Lord Jesus Christ in the most Holy Eucharist. And when you struggle and fight the forces of evil, turn to the Cross, for it is here that you shall obtain the necessary strength to fight the evil which attacks you relentlessly.

My dearest little children, I pour forth my motherly love to you this evening. For it is you who have been chosen by our Father in Heaven to lead my children into the Light, to lead my children to the Shepherd. You must remain strong. You must remain obedient. For many graces are being poured forth to you for the enlightenment, discernment and the understanding of what to do, how to do it, when to do it, and where to do it all for the honor and glory of our Father in Heaven.

Today you are my apostles, helping me preparing the way and return for my Son, Jesus Christ, to this earth from which He was born. Your journey has begun.

You, my daughter and son, will work day and night, from this period forward, not only for me, your heavenly mother, but for our Lord and Savior Jesus Christ. Do not worry about the strength to sustain you, for this will be given to you.

You must remain open to all that is being brought to you in the name of our Father in Heaven. You will proclaim the words that I have taught you that have been taught to me by my Son, Jesus Christ. As never before, you shall feel the strength and power of the Holy Spirit and your hearts shall rejoice in knowing the love that is being poured forth to you in order to carry on the work.

All of Heaven rejoices, all of Heaven has been prepared, all of Heaven now waits for the final battle.

The destruction, although devastating, is needed in order to purify an unhealthy world. Always remember, that fear is not of God, but of my Adversary.

Do not be frightened, my dear little children, for my Son is always with you.

Because I come this evening to you with a saddened heart, a broken heart, a heart that bleeds for the sins of the world, you will pray with me the Sorrowful Mysteries. And as we pray the Sorrowful Mysteries, contemplate on the pains, the suffering, the agony, that our Lord underwent for all of us.

Now all of my children will undergo suffering for our Lord and Savior Jesus Christ's return to earth. His descent will be to a New Era of Peace, love and holiness.

I ask you in urgency to go forth and proclaim what I have told you. *The time is short.* The Final Hour is upon us.

Let us now begin the Sorrowful Mysteries. Pray from the heart and soul, my dearest little children. Feel the pains my Son endured for all of us. And in union with me, your heavenly mother, hold on to my hands and let me give you the strength to carry your crosses each day."

JUNE 30, 1998

Our heavenly mother said: "O, My dearest little children, the world in which you live continues along the path of its destruction. The unhealthy lives that people live will cause many to sin and yet my children still do not heed my warning. Many have fallen away from the church that my Son has built, many still do not pray the Most Holy Rosary. Many have filled their lives with the pleasures of a meaningless sensual world, many have uncleansed souls which are not dressed in the finest of linens which I have promised to dress them in. Why my dearest little children do not my children listen? I love you my dearest daughter and son, my 'two hearts as one.'

Denise & Joseph --We love you O' heavenly mother, very much.

Our heavenly mother said: "I say these words with all my heart and soul, I am pleased to see that you have remained obedient for what I have asked you my dearest daughter and son to do. I did not promise you that there would be no pain in your lives. But you must continue to remain obedient to me, to embrace the Cross and trust in me your heavenly mother.

Never go before me and my Son as the Divine Plan becomes unraveled for you to live and unfolds before you. Remain patient, truthful, compassionate, and humble yourselves to our Lord and Savior, Jesus Christ who pours forth his love from his Sacred Heart into your hearts this evening.

I, as your heavenly mother, am so proud to know that what I have asked you to do as a mother, you respect me and follow my wishes and soon you shall see the abundance of graces that not only you have received, but will continue to receive, in the name of Our Father in Heaven.

Your struggles do not go unnoticed, and the weight of the crosses that you shall carry will become heavier in time. But trust me my dearest little children you will have the strength to carry them as my Son carried his Cross for all of us.

Even though I am not with you each day I watch over you each and every minute of your lives. I see everything, I know everything and I know what is to come. The love that you have for each other will continue to be your strength and your bond for survival.

Let us say together the Joyful Mysteries and we shall lift them up for the souls in Purgatory and for the sins of this world. And as we pray this evening I would like you to open up your hearts and souls to Our Father in Heaven who pours forth from the Holy Spirit his love unto thee as you become more and more closer to the Divine Will.

Continue on the path of holiness as you have, a path which is not smooth, a path which is narrow, steep, and bumpy. It will be your faith, your trust, and your obedience in me your heavenly mother that will carry you through these times into the New Era of Peace, where my Son's Sacred Heart and me your Immaculate Heart will triumph.

I love you my dearest, dearest, little, little children.

Let us now pray, in the Name of the Father, the Son and the Holy Spirit.

JULY 5, 1998
BIRTHDAY OF JOSEPH

We began the most Holy Rosary and our heavenly mother arrived. "We bless you in the name of Jesus Christ, if you are not of God be gone."

Joseph: "Thank you O, heavenly mother for coming this evening to celebrate my birthday during prayer with us, your two chosen children. We love you O, heavenly mother, we love you very much. Please continue to hold onto our hands as we struggle in receiving the persecutions that come our way when Satan attacks us. We are saying the prayer that you have given us to rebuke him. We love you."

Our heavenly mother said: "O, my dearest little children, let us rejoice this evening as we celebrate the birth of one of my chosen hearts. We thank our Father in heaven for the gift of life that was brought forth into this world. And now your life is to serve our Father in Heaven.

O, my dearest, dearest, little children, it gives me your heavenly mother, much happiness, much delight, much joy, in seeing that you have and continue to remain obedient to me your heavenly mother.

And, yes, my little daughter, Our Father in Heaven, the Holy Spirit, his Son, my Son, our Lord and Savior, Jesus Christ, and me, your heavenly mother, will continue to hold your hand and give you the strength to endure your crosses and pains along your journey that you have chosen to take.

Continue to hold onto my hand as I walk with you into the new Era of Peace. But today, let us celebrate for what was brought forth, as I brought forth my Son into this world, a birth of a soul, a gift from our Father in Heaven. And as I look at many of my children in this world, I see sadness, I see unhappiness, I see a world which lives by sin, a world which has cast my Son away in their lives, a world which does not recognize its Savior or me their heavenly mother.

But today, we rejoice in the birth of my little, little son. My 'two hearts as one' as we celebrate together this special day, I would like you to join me in the rosary, I would like to say one decade for my Son, and when we pray this decade, I want you to close your eyes and I want you to open up your heart and soul in thanking our Father in heaven for the gift of life, for the gift of allowing me your heavenly mother in your presence, for the gift of Our Lord and Savior, Jesus Christ which has brought eternal life to all of us.

And remember my dearest daughter and son, that a seed remains dormant until it is planted and then it gives life and bears fruit and thus it has been with you my 'two hearts as one', for you were dormant seeds until life was given to you and now you have grown into a plant and now you bear the fruits that will feed many of my children and give them the nourishment to understand and the strength to go forth.

Let us now pray to our Father in Heaven for the gift of life for all of us. In the name of the Father, the Son and the Holy Spirit. Amen."

JULY 13, 1998

Our heavenly mother said: "My dearest little children, I come this evening to you with the graces from Our Father in Heaven, it pleases me to hear you pray the Holy Rosary, it pleases me to hear you say the prayers that I have given you, the prayers which I have foretold you will touch many lives.

These prayers are special prayers, prayers given to me by Our Father in Heaven for my children. And now you will go forth on your journey and you will share these prayers and my messages for all the children of the world. Do not be frightened my dearest little ones, always remember that my Son, Jesus Christ and me your heavenly mother am always with you.

As I witness the persecutions that you undergo, continue to hold onto each other for strength, continue to get your strength by receiving the body, blood, soul and divinity of our Lord and Savior, Jesus Christ each day in the Holy Eucharist. It is here my dearest little daughter and son that you will get the strength to fight the temptations of Satan, it is here that you will get the strength to fight the persecutions that you will undergo. And in your hands my dearest little ones you hold the weapon against Satan, hold onto these Most Holy Rosaries very tightly for they will come to serve you well in these End Times.

The world in which you live is immersed in a sea of darkness, as sins spreads everywhere the light begins to diminish, evilness prevails. O, 'my two hearts as one,' the light which gives life is beginning to be filtered out by the deceptions of my Adversary, for many of my children have surrounded themselves in the simple pleasures of a meaningless world, they store their treasures of materialism rather than the treasures of prayer.

But the light my dearest little daughter and son shall never go out and it shall serve as a means to show the way to follow, the way to eternal salvation. Continue to remain obedient and trusting in me your heavenly mother, Our Lord and Savior, Jesus Christ, and Our Father in Heaven the Creator. Close your eyes my dearest little children as I open up my Immaculate Heart, feel the love flow into your heart, feel my warmth now enter into you. Feel the warmth now begin to increase within your heart and soul, feel my motherly love wrap around your heart and soul.

I am Coredemptrix of all graces, graces bestowed upon me by Our Father in Heaven, through my Son, Jesus Christ. And as I stand before you, I ask you my dearest little ones to go forth and praise thy Father's Name. Do not be frightened, do not be worried for we always go before you preparing the way. And remember that through God all things are made possible.

Let us pray the Most Holy Rosary now and you my dearest little daughter will lead us in the Joyful Mysteries, the Mysteries which have found favor in your heart, and soul. I ask you as your mother to lead me and my Son in the Holy Rosary for our Lord and Savior, Jesus Christ."

JULY 25, 1998

We begin the Joyful Mysteries. Our heavenly mother arrives during the third mystery. "We bless you O, heavenly mother, in the name of the Father the Son and the Holy Spirit, if you are not of God be gone."

Heavenly mother: "O, My beloved little children, through the graces of Our Father in Heaven, I come to you this evening to join you in prayer. As I witness in Heaven your struggles, you must never forget that I, your heavenly mother and my Son, our Lord and Savior, Jesus Christ are always with you. But you must remain open in receiving our love and strength.

Feel my motherly love now enter into you as I pour forth my love, let it fill your hearts and souls. Close your eyes my dearest little children, there is much tension within you, release this tension and lift it up into Heaven, feel my motherly love flow within you. Feel your heart jump with joy in knowing that Heaven now lives within you and always will be with you.

My dearest little daughter and son, there is much persecution that not only continues now, but will continue in the future. You must stand your ground as a gallant soldier as I have told you and fight this battle with me, your heavenly mother. Confusion, fear, doubt, hatred is not of my Son or Our Father in Heaven, but of my Adversary which infiltrates your mind. You must rebuke him as I have foretold you. You must use your Holy Water, for this you have not been doing. You must form the shield of protection around you at all times as we enter into the critical point of the End Times. O, my dearest little daughter and son, my heart weeps in sorrow to see you suffer, but you must remain strong, you must trust in me, your heavenly mother, and above all you must remain obedient to the will of me, your heavenly mother. But yet you, my son, continue to struggle. You fail at times to embrace the cross for your strength. Your obedience wavers back and forth which concerns me, your heavenly mother. And you, my daughter, when you see him in this state, it is up to you to hold onto him tight and to guide him. As I have foretold you, you are the strongest of the 'two hearts as one.' Do not place doubt in your strength, my dearest daughter, for this is caused by the confusion of my

Adversary who weakens you. Let us now pray, as you have, the Joyful Mysteries. And you, my dearest little daughter, will lead us as you have. I have come to you this evening to pray and give you strength. This is my evening with you, rejoice and be glad. And now, my dearest little daughter, I, your heavenly mother and my Son, will pray with you both.

AUGUST 10, 1998

Our heavenly mother said: "My dearest little children my heart weeps in much sorrow, as I look upon this world, many of my children are lost. Many of my children are being deceived by my Adversary, and remain in the state of confusion, not knowing the ways to turn. They have lost their direction and cannot see the light, The Eternal Light.

O, my dearest little 'two hearts as one,' can you not see? Look around you and there you will witness what I am telling you. You must go forth my, dearest little children, and proclaim the word of God as I have taught you. Remain focused on the Cross, remember my teachings, for they will become the tools for you to use in this the final hour, the final battle for souls.

You must remain strong my dearest daughter and son. Your strength shall come from the faith that you place in my Son, Our Lord and Savior Jesus Christ. It shall be replenished when you receive the Holy Eucharist, the Body, Blood, Soul and Divinity of Our Lord and Savior Jesus Christ.

As you look around, you see a world that is enveloped in darkness, do not become frightened for no harm shall come to you. You will remain in the mantle of my protection.

And as I have foretold you, you shall undergo persecutions and sufferings for the sins of the world. I have not promised you that you shall not receive these persecutions and sufferings. I ask you to embrace them with your love. And when doubt and confusion enter into your minds, remember what I have told you, focus on the cross, embrace the cross, and use your Holy Water. Use the weapons that I have given to you.

In this the final hour, Satan will attack you relentlessly. You will fight him. Continue to remain strong, for the attacks will become greater, and greater and greater as you do the work of my Son. He wishes to destroy you both, my dearest little daughter and son.

Always remember, that the power given to you is from God, and no power is greater than the power of your Creator. If you concentrate on Our Father in Heaven, you will feel his power enter into your heart and soul, giving you the strength to fight in this the Final Battle. And yes, my dearest daughter and son, I see you both struggle, but I am always with you. You must call upon me often, for my strength and guidance. Continue to remain obedient as I have requested you. Obedience is a true virtue and the *most important* virtue in these the End Times. You will remain obedient for me Your Heavenly Mother.

It gives me much joy, my dearest little daughter and son, to be here with my 'two hearts as one.' Feel my presence and open up your heart and soul. Allow the love of your heavenly mother to enter into you. Close your eyes, my dearest children. Feel the peace, feel the peace that I bring from heaven. Feel your heart and soul being lifted. Allow my motherly love to enter into you.

AUGUST 13, 1998

Denise, Joseph, and Father George Lukaczyk are present. Our Heavenly Mother arrives, we bless her in the name of the Father the Son and the Holy Spirit, "...if you are not of God be gone."

Denise says, "She is present, Father George."

Our heavenly mother said: "O, my beloved children, I send forth my motherly love to you this evening. I come to you with a heavy heart, for many of my children still live in darkness of a sensual world, a world in which my Adversary has deceived many. The darkness envelopes the world and the light becomes diminished. Many of my children have rejected God and have turned to a materialistic world.

The Remnant few, whose faith continues, whose prayers continue, have brought and continue to bring joy to my Son and our Father in Heaven.

I love you, my dearest little children. I will always love you with my motherly love and watch over you. But the dangers which lie ahead, my children, must be warned. They can not continue on the path that they have chosen, a unholy path. Can they not see the many signs being given to them by our Heavenly Father? In these good times in which they live, they reject these signs, their faith diminishes. They must continue to pray, pray, ***pray*** the Holy Rosary! They must come back to ***trust***, trust in our Father in Heaven and our Lord and Savior, Jesus Christ.

O, my dearest little children, feel my motherly love being poured forth from My Immaculate Heart unto thee. I am preparing my children for the greatest event in history, which will soon unfold. Then all shall bear witness and know there is but One God, our Creator. Through Him all things are made possible.

My wound, that I sustained at the foot of the Cross, continues to weep. But the darkness will soon give way to the Light, and a New Dawn Day will spring forth, where its fruits shall flourish and the flowers will blossom, and in the new paradise, the new Era of Peace, my Son shall descend in His Glory.

Many of my beloved priests have fallen victim to my Adversary's deceitful ways and lead the flock along the unholy path. Few have remained obedient and faithful. They continue to deny our Lord and Savior, Jesus Christ, just as the Apostles denied Him when He remained alone on that Friday, suffering for our Sins. But yet, at the foot of the Cross, remained the faithful.

We must continue to pray for my beloved priests and bishops, who wander aimlessly away from my Son's Church and lead their flocks away from God.

Blessed are you, my beloved priest, whose faith has remained obedient in the most difficult of times. You have stood your ground during persecutions. Blessed are you, for many graces fall upon you from my Son, our Lord and Savior, Jesus Christ. For you are of the Remnant Few, for which I, your Heavenly Mother, speak.

The faith which radiates from your soul is felt by those who follow you. You represent my Son's Church well. The deep love you have for our Lord and Savior emanates a light which has touched many.

I send forth my motherly graces and love unto thee. And thus you are blessed, my beloved priest. And thus you are chosen, and you serve well.

Continue on your holy path, continue to lead, continue to teach, continue to show my children who come to you, the way of the Lord. The Holy Spirit rests upon you. Blessed are you amongst my children. You were blessed to see the signs given to you from Heaven. But remember, blessed are they who believe and do not see.

You have been chosen from the Most High, to fill your mission for which you were chosen. Keep my "two hearts as one" close to you. There shall be many other signs given to you. I ask you, as I do my dearest daughter and son, to remain open with innocence, so that these signs can be discerned and you shall know that they are of Heaven.

Many graces my Son pours forth to thee in helping my dear little children fulfill their divine mission. What you have seen, what you have heard, and what you are hearing, is divine.

Join me now as we pray the Most Holy Rosary. We shall say the Glorious Mysteries. No, we shall finish the Glorious Mysteries. We have four more Hail Marys to say and we shall say the Joyful Mysteries, and I shall teach you the Joyful Mysteries as I, your Heavenly Mother, have lived them."

SEPTEMBER 3, 1998

"We love you O, heavenly mother and missed you very much. And you live within our hearts and soul each day. We love you."

Our heavenly mother said: "My dearest daughter, always remember that I am always with you and my son. I always look upon you. I know all your actions, those whom you interact with, what is said to you and what you say and act to others. My love is always with you both, my 'two hearts as one.' You must never forget that.

As my heart is in union with my Son's Heart, my heart is in union with your hearts. And as one, we shall triumph together in these, the End Times. It is through the graces of the Heavenly Father that I am here this evening with you. We must always respect our Father in Heaven, for it is through Him and with Him that all things are made possible.

My dearest little children, as I speak to you the world is on the brink of economic crisis. I have foretold you this and it shall come to being. It is here that the Anti-Christ shall make himself known. You must be prepared, my dearest little children, for the times of which I have spoken to you privately are now about to be unveiled to all my children of the world. Look at the natural disasters that have happened to your country, and yet my children still have remained blinded by the ways that they have chosen to live.

Disasters will increase in intensity, lives will be taken. *Why* have my children not listened to my pleas? Why have my children turned *against* their God?!

My Son, our Lord and Savior Jesus Christ, has shown us the way that we must follow. Yet many of my children follow their own ways to satisfy their own pleasures. **They will soon come to know that everything that has been given to them has been through our Father in Heaven. And this will now be taken away from them; things that they have worked so hard for in their lives will be nothing. What they should have placed and stored their treasures in, is in their faith, trust and obedience to our Father in Heaven.**

Yesterday you learned that the seed gives way to a plant. And the plant is cultivated by Heaven. And it bears fruits. But the plant must be willing to accept what has been given to it by its gardener.

A plant is recognized by the fruits it bears, and today many bad fruits appear on many plants, which have caused contamination of the good fruits born by the Remnant few.

I have come here this evening, my 'two hearts as one,' to pray with you, to pray for what is about to happen, to pray for the souls of my children. You must remain strong as you have.

I am proud of you, my little daughter and son, for the strength that you have shown in fighting the temptations of Satan, the confusion, the doubt, that my adversary inflicts upon you each day. And as each day passes you gain strength to fight back. Your fear becomes less, because you know that fear is not of God. You now know that the power of God gives you the strength to fight my adversary. Continue to remain strong and focus on the Cross, the sign of your salvation and redemption.

In the days to come my adversary will attack you more and more and more. You are to rebuke him in the name of our Lord and Savior, Jesus Christ. Do not allow him to cause confusion and doubt in your lives. Always place your trust in me, your heavenly mother, and all that I have said will come true.

Pray with me, dearest little children, pray with me the Holy Rosary. Let us pray the Joyful Mysteries. And when we pray, remember what I have taught you.

Let us begin to pray now. In the Name of the Father, Son and Holy Spirit. Amen."

SEPTEMBER 13, 1998

O, heavenly mother, we bless you in the name of the Father, the Son and the Holy Spirit. If you are not of God, be gone. We bless her with Holy Water.

Our heavenly mother arrived while we were saying the Holy Rosary.

"My dearest daughter and son, I see that you have brought me many religious articles. My heart is filled with joy in seeing that my children wish me to bless them in my name and in my Son's name, and in the Father's name.

But this evening I come to you with a heavy heart for the final hour has come upon this world which has been led by my adversary along the roads of sinfulness. And many of my children have been deceived and live lives of sin. Many of my children have fallen away from the true belief, the true faith that my Son had established for all his peoples. And I ask you to look around you and what do you see? You see confusion, for many of my children live in confusion. But yet they have accepted these ways as normal ways in their lives, but today a sinful way has been chosen over the rightful way of love, peace and happiness.

And as these heavenly signs are given to you they are to remind you that there is one Divine Being and that is of Our Father in heaven, and these signs shall increase in number and their intensity shall also increase.

And every knee shall bend in time in realizing that the Father is the Creator and the Alpha, the Omega the beginning and the end to all. The time has now come for the Triumph of my Immaculate Heart and the defeat of my adversary, but yet much pain and suffering will my children undergo for the purification.

Many of my beloved priests live sinful lives in causing the apostasy that exists in my Son's church resulting in the confusion of his flock for many have been driven away from my Son's church. And as the cup overflows with the blood that my Son shed on Calvary, the price that my children must pay will be severe.

And I ask you, my dearest children, to pray, pray, pray from your hearts and souls, for the times ahead will be difficult, the times ahead will be painful. Always remember to focus on the Cross the sign of your salvation. Embrace the Cross and hold on to it tightly in these the End Times. For many of my children are lost and can not find nor see the way, but yet when I, your heavenly mother, show them the way they refuse to believe and accept the divine path of holiness.

Please my dearest daughter and son, let us pray the most Holy Rosary, and let us say the last two Hail Mary's in the completion of the Mystery in which you had begun. Always remember the souls in Purgatory that we must continue to pray for their salvation. Let us now begin."

After the rosary she says:

"My dearest daughter and son, let us pray together the Glorious Mysteries. I choose this mystery this evening because they clearly represent the events that are about to unfold upon this world. Let us now begin and pray the Glorious Mysteries for our Lord and Savior, Jesus Christ and Our Father in Heaven, praising Them in thanksgiving for the love that They give to each and every one of my children, a love that is everlasting, and a love that is infinite. Let us now begin."

Fourteen Special Prayers

PRAYERS GIVEN TO US
BY OUR HEAVENLY MOTHER
FOR US TO PRAY WITH HER
WHEN SHE COMES

(1)

Jesus, our most loving Redeemer, You came to enlighten the world with Your teachings. Graciously accept my prayers which I dedicate to You. Protect me, guard and keep me in holy fear, in peace and in the harmony of Your Love. Conform me into Your divine Form, and may I attain eternal happiness always through Thee.
Amen.

(2)

Lord, I pray that You are always with me, and protect me from the snares of the enemy. Let Your Holy Angles dwell upon me and preserve in me Your Peace and Love. As I humbly worship You with all my heart and soul, let Your blessings be always upon me, in the Name of the Father, Son and Holy Spirit.
Amen.

(3)

O, My Lord Jesus Christ, the true Lamb that takes away the sins of the world, through Thy Mercy, forgive me for my sins and by Thy sacred passion, preserve me this day from all sin and evil. I offer myself entirely as a sacrifice of love, which Thou offered for me on the Cross. Accept me, my Lord in Your hands, and surround me each day with Your Love, Peace and compassion.
Amen.

(4)

Lord, You are the Shepherd who provides for all. Let the Holy Spirit descend upon me each day for enlightenment, discernment and the virtues I will need for strength and courage. Let Your Light of Love, Mercy and Spirit shine within my soul. Fill my grieving heart with Your joy and holiness. As I humble myself to receive You, purify and heal me always to the Will of the Father, Son and Holy Spirit.
Amen.

(5)

Lord Jesus Christ, the true God of pure Love and compassion, I glorify You with humble obedience. Open my heart to receive Your tender Love. Take away my sinfulness and transform me to receive Life, healing and forgiveness through You. Fill me with Your Spirit, so that I may treasure Your Kingdom within my soul. And may Your Peace, Mercy and blessings always remain with me.
Amen.

(6)

Loving Father, You are the source of all wisdom and truth. Help me to recognize my sinfulness and to admit to my faults. Give me the strength to acknowledge and confess my sins and the graces to overcome them. Guide me and protect me, cleanse me and make me pleasing to You, so that I may serve You with humility and love. Dear Father, embrace me with Your loving arms of Mercy and bless me each day in the Name of the Father, Son and Holy Spirit.
Amen.

(7)

Lord Jesus Christ, You were sent by the Father, as an offering for our sins. May Your Spirit enlighten and strengthen me, to preserve in my daily trials. I totally surrender myself to You, Lord, to receive Your Peace, Joy, Hope and divine Love. Prepare me each day with humble obedience, in order to attain eternal salvation in Your Kingdom and meet our Father in Heaven. Amen.

(8)

O, my beloved Jesus Christ, through our most Holy Mother, the Blessed Virgin Mary, I totally surrender myself to Your Divine Will. Let the Holy Spirit shower me with His gifts and protect me from the deceptions of the Evil One. Give me the strength, graces and courage to grow in holiness, and be united with Your Sacred and Merciful Heart. Through Your Resurrection, may I come into my glory with the Father, Son and Holy Spirit. Amen.

(9)

Father in Heaven, You are the divine Master. Through Baptism, You purified my heart and soul. Give me the wisdom to grow in faith, trust and humility, so that I may be filled with Your sanctifying grace. Let each morning be a new beginning in my preparation, to bear the fruits of virtues, born by the Holy Spirit, so that I may dwell in the garden of Your divine Will. Blessed be forever, the God and Father of our Lord and Savior Jesus Christ.
Amen.

(10)

O, Heavenly Father, You created me to the glory of Thy name. Give me the strength and courage to serve You always, and as I remain hidden within Your bosom, let my obedience, perseverance and humbleness, open my heart to receive the power of forgiveness, in cleansing my soul, so that I may be filled with Thy divine Love. And through Thy most Sacred and Merciful Heart, shower me always with Thy most Holy Trinity, Father, Son and Holy Spirit.
Amen.

(11)

O, My Lord Jesus Christ, the Truth and Way to eternal Light, let the Holy Spirit fill me with His strength, so that I may endure the crosses You give me each day. And as I unite my sufferings and pains with You on the cross, let Your graces be released to free those from the sins of darkness. And may I always embrace the Love of our Heavenly Father and the Peace of His Son, our Lord Jesus Christ.

Amen.

(12)

Most Holy Trinity, through our Blessed Heavenly Mother, protect and strengthen me from the temptations of Satan. And as I place my complete trust in You, let the Light, Truth and Way of my salvation continue to lead me towards the path of holiness. And may the love of our Heavenly Mother, heal me always and lead me into the Kingdom of her Son, where I will bask in the eternal glory of the Father, Son and Holy Spirit.

Amen.

(13)

O, Father in Heaven, our Creator, as my soul reaches out, fill it with the compassion and nourishing presence of Our Lord and Savior, Jesus Christ. And as I completely immerse myself in His Mercy, grace me with Your forgiveness for my sins and manifest my spiritual qualities to the divine Will of the Father, Son and Holy Spirit, where I may live in union with Them for Eternity.

Amen.

(14)

O, Heavenly Father, blessed be Thy Name, for through the graces You have blessed us with our Guardian Angels, who watch over us each day and each night, and as we pray, let our love, peace and compassion, become united as one with theirs, in union with our Lord and Savior, Jesus Christ and teach us O, Guardian Angels to become humble and obedient to receiving our Father's divine Will, and the Love of our Lord and Savior, Jesus Christ, and may we always be blessed in union with the Holy Trinity, Father, Son and Holy Spirit.

Amen.

The Blessed Mother's Prayers given to Denise and Joseph

JUNE 13, 1997

O, heavenly mother, should we be saying special prayers to our Guardian Angels who are so very special to us?

Heavenly mother: "My dearest daughter, you should always delight not only your Guardian Angels, who wait to be called to join you in prayer, but the entire cohort of Angels in Heaven, who will join you in prayer. When you pray my daughter, pray like this:

O, Angels of Heaven, as I kneel before our Lord Jesus Christ, join me in prayer. As we pray, let our prayers in union with our Lord and heavenly mother, be lifted to our Father in Heaven. O, Guardian Angel, my protector, you have been given to me through the Father, to watch over me until I join you in Paradise. Pray with me each day, love me each day, and lead me to holiness. Amen."

JULY 13, 1997

Dearest heavenly mother, could you please give us a special prayer that we could say when we receive the Body and Blood of your Son, our Lord and Savior, Jesus Christ, as we both cherish very much the Angel prayer that you have given us?

Heavenly mother: "My daughter and son, in receiving Holy Communion, you truly are receiving the Body and Blood of my Son and your Savior, Jesus Christ. Remember to always pay reverence to Him during Communion. My heart leaps with joy to see you kneel in receiving His precious Body and Blood, for so few of my children pay such reverence to Him as you, my chosen children. Your hearts leap with joy and become filled with His Love in receiving Him. Because of your obedience and reverence, when you receive Holy Communion pray like this.

My Divine Lord, I offer this Holy Communion to atone for my sinfulness and to receive the graces necessary to obtain eternal salvation and perseverance to the end. Prepare me to receive Thy Body, Blood, Soul and Divinity as food to nourish my soul. I love Thee with my whole heart and desire to live and die in Thy holy love. Amen."

AUGUST 15, 1997 - FEAST OF THE ASSUMPTION

O, heavenly mother, we would like to say a prayer to all the Saints and Apostles, could you please help us with a prayer?

Heavenly mother: "When you pray my daughter and son, pray like this, this prayer you will recite each night in prayer:

O, Father in Heaven, grace those chosen who have given and dedicated their entire life to Your Divine Will, and as they serve You each day with all of their heart, all of their love and all of their soul, guide them through the Holy Spirit so that they may understand Your ways and means to eternal salvation, and may the Light of eternity always shine upon them until they come into their glory in the presence of Your Son, Jesus Christ, where they shall live and reign forever. Amen."

O, heavenly mother, before you leave us tonight, could you please grace our rosary beads for us?

"My daughter and son, hold forth your beads and listen what I say for you, my son and daughter, when I grace these special holy objects:

Through the power invested in me through our Father, I bless and grace these holy objects and may the Holy Spirit descend upon them and remain with them and may my graces continue to shower my children forever. Amen."

SEPTEMBER 13, 1997

Joseph gave me a beautiful ring, to honor the Mission we accepted for God the Father. The ring is an oval topaz with a cross etched into the stone. I asked our heavenly mother to give me a prayer and to place her special graces on this ring.

Heavenly mother: "My dearest daughter, In the name of the Father, the Son and the Holy Spirit .

O, Father in Heaven, grace this ring as a sign of the cross as a reminder of our salvation into Thy Kingdom of Heaven. Pour forth Thy love unto my daughter, and when she gazes upon this ring which she shall wear day and night, let it remind her of my Son, our Lord and Savior Jesus Christ, and His death on the Cross, and let this love fill her soul each time and give her the strength to endure her daily trials and let Thy Holy Spirit descend upon her and protect her from my Adversary and his cohorts and continue to grace her with Your love and forgiveness until she joins us in Thy Kingdom of Heaven. And so with the power invested in me through You, our Father in Heaven, I bless this ring, in the Name of the Father, thy Son, and thy Holy Spirit. Amen."

"And, my dearest daughter, I seal that prayer with my kiss, and each night when you close your eyes and I place my kiss on your forehead, let it remind you of this very special prayer which will rest upon you for Eternity."

SEPTEMBER 20, 1997

FOR DENISE TO BEAR WITNESS TO HER

Heavenly mother: "Open thy hands and pour forth to thy Father in Heaven, gaze upon His beauty for He is your Creator:

Father in Heaven, through Thy Love, you made me as an image of You, and now we are blessed with Your graces to bear witness to our heavenly mother, I send forth from my heart and soul to You, in thanking You for being our Father in Heaven, our Creator, and through Your power given to our heavenly mother, bless us in the Name of the Father, the Son, and Thy Holy Spirit. Amen."

OCTOBER 13, 1997

HOLY SPIRIT PRAYER

"O, my beloved Father, You grace me with Your Love and presence by allowing the Holy Spirit to enter my soul. And, as I rest in thy peace, let Your presence kindle the everlasting flame of my love for You in my soul forever, and may it become the everlasting light of my salvation into Thy Kingdom of Heaven. Amen."

NOVEMBER 13, 1997

PRAYER FROM OUR HEAVENLY MOTHER FOR JOSEPH'S NEW HOME

O, heavenly mother, this being a new house for Joseph, we would like you to bless it with your motherly blessings.

Heavenly mother: "My beloved daughter, it gives me much pleasure and honor as your heavenly mother to bless this house, for this house is truly a blessed place. Always remember that, for the ground that you stand on is holy. And so blessed are you, my dear children, for you are holy children, for if this were not true I would not speak the truth, and if this were not so, you would not be given all that you have been given, and you would not have seen all that you have seen or all that you are about to see. We will say a prayer together in the blessings for this house, your house, and my house, and our Lord and Savior, Jesus Christ's house, for it is here in this room He lives, His Body, Blood, Soul and Divinity, the true Presence of my Son.

O, Heavenly Father, bless this house for your chosen children, let Your graces fall from Heaven, and form a shield to protect this house from Satan and all his evil spirits. And may Your Divine Love, Peace and happiness remain and flow in each of these rooms for those who enter this house will be blessed by You, our Heavenly Father, and through the graces and power of the Holy Trinity, bless this house in the Name of the Father, the Son and the Holy Spirit. Amen."

NOVEMBER 13, 1997

Before our heavenly mother left us during prayer on this day she said:

"Before I leave you, my children, I will give you a prayer from my heart to your heart, a prayer that I will say before you that I have never said before:

O, my Lord, my Son, Jesus Christ, grant me your heavenly mother, my request to bless my chosen children, and through Thy mercy, forgive them for their sins, and through Thy blessings fill them with Your love, peace, and compassion. And let Your presence live within them, and their love within You, and do not forsake them, for they are chosen children, and as Your heavenly mother, embrace them with Your love and protect them with Your might and power against the Adversary, and lead them to holiness. And on their journey give them the food of the Holy Spirit so that they may understand, discern and obtain the wisdom to know what is of God and from God and to lead them to Our Father in Heaven. Amen."

DECEMBER 13, 1997

For Denise's birthday, December 7, 1997, a necklace with the heavenly mother and the infant Jesus was given to her. Denise asked our heavenly mother to place her graces upon this special necklace. Our heavenly mother said:

"O, Father in Heaven, through Thy Love, you have created this beautiful child. Bless her with Your divine Love and let Thy graces pour forth through Thy hand unto my hands unto her. And bless her and this gift through the power of my Beloved Spouse, the Holy Spirit, In the Name of the Father, Son and Holy Spirit. Amen."

DECEMBER 13, 1997

This was a prayer given to Denise from our heavenly mother. Deborah, the twin sister of Denise, bought Denise and herself a ring with a gold cross on it. Denise asked our heavenly mother to place her graces on them. Denise extended her hand with the rings on them.

"O, Holy Spirit, my Beloved Spouse, descend upon these rings the salvation of my children's faith into the Promised Land. And through the powers invested in me, through God, our Heavenly Father, I bless with my Motherly love, in the name of the Father Son, and Holy Spirit. Amen. And I pour forth my Motherly love from my Immaculate Heart to the crosses carried by my Son, your Redemption and Salvation forever. Amen."

JANUARY 5, 1998

Before our heavenly mother left us after an evening of prayer, she said: "Before I leave you, my children, I shall grace you with a prayer which you shall repeat after me. Open up your hands and receive my love and that of my Spouse, the Holy Spirit:

O, Heavenly Father, the journey has begun for my chosen children, a gift from you to me. And as my Spouse overshadows them, give them the strength to endure their trials and persecutions.

Give them the enlightenment, discernment and knowledge to proclaim the Word of God. And fill their weary souls with Your love and strength and may the Sacred Heart of Your beloved Son, Jesus Christ, become the temple within their souls, and the rays of my love shine forth from my heart. Let its warmth and tenderness embrace them forever. Amen."

JANUARY 13, 1998

Denise received two gifts from Joseph's sister, Shirley Soucy. One was a necklace with the Holy Spirit on it, the other was a pair of Rosary beads that she picked up in Rome, and was blessed by the Pope. She asked the heavenly mother to bless them.

"O, Father in Heaven, if it be thy Will, let thy Holy Spirit, my beloved Spouse descend upon these holy objects and my children, and bless them with Thy Heavenly Love, and protect them with Thy strength and guide them in the End Times, and protect them from the Evil One. I bless you in the Name of the Father, Son, and Holy Spirit. Amen."

JANUARY 13, 1998

This prayer was given to us by our heavenly mother. She said to us:

"My daughter and my son, each night when you rest, I place my Motherly kiss upon your forehead and I gaze up to Heaven and say:

O, Father in Heaven, bless this child, for his day is done and give him the strength tomorrow to do 'Thy Will be done,' but let his soul rest this night and give him Peace in your Love. Amen."

"O, Father in Heaven, bless this child for her day is done and give her the strength tomorrow, to do 'Thy Will be done,' but let her soul rest this night and give her Peace in Your Love. Amen."

She then said to us: "For that is why, my dear children, you are highly favored by Our Father in Heaven, for you do His work. And our work shall never end, for many of the sheep still wander in darkness and have lost the Shepherd. Many cannot see the light, for the light has been covered by the deceptions of the Evil One. But do not be discouraged, my dear little children, for we shall triumph together. And as a rose brings sweetness, so too shall my victory bring sweetness to those faithful, the remnant few who remain obedient to my Son, our Lord and Savior Jesus Christ, who suffered on the cross for our sins."

JANUARY 13, 1998

A statue of Saint Kateri Tekakwitha that was given as a gift to Joseph and Denise was weeping holy oils prior to our heavenly mother's apparition. We asked her to please pour forth her blessing upon this statue for the holy room. She said to us,

"My beloved daughter and son, each object in this room is holy, for you stand on holy ground. A statue cannot weep unless it is blessed by Heaven, and does it pour forth Heaven's gift? I shall bless this statue, but always remember what I have foretold, it must also be blessed by my Beloved Priests. Hold forth the statue and repeat these words my children:

O, Holy Spirit, my beloved Spouse, bless this statue, with the graces of our Father in Heaven, and the mercy and sacredness of my Son, our Lord and Savior Jesus Christ. And may the tears that pour forth, bring graces upon those it touches, and may it heal the souls that remain darkened, and hidden, and let Thy sun shine forth and its new day be dawn and gift this new life. And may the graces of the Holy Trinity bless this statue in the Name of the Father, the Son and the Holy Spirit. Amen."

JANUARY 13, 1998

We had a guest for a speaking engagement, and he joined us in prayer with our heavenly mother. We asked our heavenly mother to give him a special prayer for him to say before his speaking engagements to proclaim the Word of God. Our heavenly mother gave him a beautiful prayer:

"O, Father in Heaven, open up my heart and soul, and let Thy Spirit descend unto me. And as You fill me with Your graces, let it flow from within my heart and soul, to those before me, and let Thy words rest upon them and touch their hearts and begin to shed light upon their souls, and let the Holy Spirit fill this room and open up their minds to receiving Thy words that you have given me. And let Thy Love, Peace, Joy, and the happiness fill their hearts and soul and continue to grow as they leave. And let Thy Light that shines forth show them the way on the path to holiness and continue to lead them to the Day of the Lord. And I thank You, Father, for giving me the gift of life and I thank You for giving me the invitation to saying 'yes.' And I embrace the 'yes' with all my heart, with all my soul, and with all my love, for I love Thee. And I thank You for giving me our Lord and Savior Jesus Christ as a sacrifice for our sins, so that I may have everlasting Life in Thy Kingdom of Heaven. Amen."

JANUARY 21, 1998

During prayer, our heavenly mother appeared to us as we asked that some Miraculous Medals be blessed. These medals are for immediate family members.

"I, the Immaculate Virgin, the Mother of our Lord and Savior Jesus Christ, pour forth my blessing unto these medals. I grace them with my Motherly love and through the power of Our Father in Heaven, may my beloved Spouse descend upon these medals, giving them the virtues of Life. For those who wear this medal shall humble themselves before our Lord and Savior, Jesus Christ, whose Love, Peace, Joy and Holiness shall pour forth unto them; whose hearts will come to know the Presence of my Son. And may their souls be strengthened through the End Times, and may they discern right from wrong, and may they be protected from the temptations of the Evil One. And I bless them in the Name of the Father, the Son and The Holy Spirit. Amen."

FEBRUARY 13, 1998

We asked our heavenly mother to bless some medals that we purchased. She also reminded us that we must also have these holy objects blessed by her beloved priests:

"O, Father in Heaven, through Thy graces, grant me, the Mother of Your Son, Our Lord and Savior, Jesus Christ, through the power of my beloved Spouse, the Holy Spirit, to send forth upon these holy objects, my graces, my love; and may these holy objects protect those who wear them, and give them the love from our Father in Heaven to nourish their hearts and souls, so that they may give these to others. And through 'Thy Will be done,' bless these objects in the Name of the Father, the Son and the Holy Spirit. Amen."

FEBRUARY 17, 1998

During prayer, our heavenly mother appeared to us. Before she left us on this evening, we asked her to bless us before she ascended into Heaven. She said:

"Let your hearts and souls open to the fullest as I now give you my blessings before leaving:

O, Creator of Heaven and Earth, let the Holy Spirit rest upon my children's souls, and as they journey along their path of holiness; let the rein of wisdom wet their tongues and quench their thirst and may the Peace, Love, and Joy fill them always to the greater glory of Our Lord and Savior, Jesus Christ. And let us, in union with His sufferings on the Cross, forgive all my children of their sins and bring them back on the road to holiness and Eternal Salvation into Thy Kingdom of the new Era of Peace. Amen."

MARCH 10, 1998

Our heavenly mother appeared to us and, during prayer, she gave us a prayer during this Lenten season:

"On this Lenten season, open up your souls and your hearts to ask for forgiveness and to repent for your sins and to receive the graces and mercy of Our Lord and Savior, Jesus Christ. Wash your souls, clean and prepare them for fasting to sustain the pains of His crucifixion and to glorify His risen Body for the Life that brings forth our souls into His Heavenly Kingdom. And may His Love, Peace, and Mercy continue to guide you and lead you to the Day of the Lord. May the Holy Spirit descend upon you to fulfill our Father's Divine Plan. May my Motherly Love of my Immaculate Heart and the Sacred Heart of my Son, continue to nourish you to bear thy fruits of all my children and lead them on the path of holiness, a journey to sustain Life everlasting, into Thy Kingdom of Heaven. Amen."

MARCH 11, 1998

While Joseph was in prayer, our heavenly mother appeared to him and said:

"Hail to the Guardian in doctrine of divine Beacon of Truth, that shall never fail to shine. Error shall never against Him prevail and your faith shall not fail. For you are showered with the graces of perseverance in the good work you have undertaken. Pray, pray, pray much, my dear child, and make sacrifices for sinners. Amen."

MARCH 13, 1998

During prayer with our heavenly mother, Denise had asked our heavenly mother for a prayer for her daughter, Chanel's birthday, who had turned 16 on this day.   Our heavenly mother said:

"My beloved daughter, as a chosen child you will grace your child through me. I will pour forth a prayer for you. For you will recite this prayer to her, and when you do so, you will pour forth my love and graces unto her. And when you pray with her, you will cleanse your hands in Holy Water. You will ask our Father in heaven to cleanse you of all your sins, and you will ask him to let the Holy Spirit descend upon you. You will then pray like this:

O, Father in Heaven, through Your graces and Mercy, bless this child I set my hands upon, hands that were cleansed through the Blood that Your Son shed for us on Mount Calvary. Pour forth Your Love unto this child, protect this child along her journey, watch over this child each day and let the Holy Spirit guide this child along the path of holiness to obtain a life of eternal salvation into the Promised Land. And as You have given life through a soul, give this soul the Light to see the Day of our Lord, and let this light shine forth from her heart and soul to You, O, Father in Heaven, and to Your Son, our Lord and Savior, Jesus Christ. For the Light will represent the love she has for those who have given her life and those who give her Eternal Life. Amen."

MARCH 13, 1998

Our heavenly mother gives us a prayer for our family members' items that she requested they purchase to prepare them for the End Times:

"In the Name of the Father, the Son and the Holy Spirit. Amen. O, Heavenly Father, as we begin our exile into these places of safe haven, may these articles which You have requested, be blessed, graced and covered with the Blood of Your Son, our Lord and Savior, Jesus Christ. And may each article be blessed by Thy Holy Spirit so that the wisdom, knowledge and understandings be given to those whom it touches, so that they may come to know the Word of God, and may the graces that now flow from my hands unto these articles give them the fruits to nourish their souls, so that they may bear the fruits for others to see. And may these articles give them the comfort, protection and love of you O, Heavenly Father. And as I raise my hands, let the love of You, O, Heavenly Father, through Your Son, our Lord and Savior, Jesus Christ, enter into my Immaculate Heart and let Thy rays shine forth unto these articles. Fill them with my Motherly Love and may the Holy Spirit in union with my Son our Lord and Savior, Jesus Christ through Our Father in Heaven, bless these articles in the Name of the Father, the Son and the Holy Spirit. Amen."

MARCH 13, 1998

Per the request of our heavenly mother, we purchased Benedictine medals for the children of our families. We asked our heavenly mother to bless these medals before giving them to the children:

"In the Name of the Father, the Son and the Holy Spirit, Amen. Through the graces of our Father in Heaven, may these medals, which are to be worn by my children, protect them from the deceptions and temptations of Satan. And may these medals remind them that the presence of our Lord and Savior, Jesus Christ exists in each of His children who remain obedient and reverent to Him. They shall open their hearts and souls, and love Him as their Savior. And each day they must recite the Our Father in the morning before their day has begun, and they must thank the Father in Heaven for a new day's dawn. And they must bless themselves with Holy Water, in the Name of the Father, the Son, and the Holy Spirit, and they must kiss the medal before they begin their day. For this will give them the shield of protection that they will need. They must wear this medal at all times, never to remove it, you must tell them, my children, the importance of which I speak. Amen."

APRIL 9, 1998   GOOD FRIDAY

Our heavenly mother came to us on Good Friday to prepare us for the crucifixion of our Lord and Savior, Jesus Christ. She said to us:

"At the hour of 3:00 p.m., in recognition of my Son's death, you shall go into adoration for one hour, you shall remain in silent prayer, you shall concentrate on His death on the Cross, you shall focus on my Son, Our Lord and Savior, Jesus Christ, His death for all of us. At the end of adoration you shall drink of the cup of wine, and before you eat the unleavened bread or drink of the cup, you shall recite this prayer:

O, Father in Heaven, in the glory of Thy Name, through Your Son, our Lord and Savior, Jesus Christ, through His agony and pain, and through His death on the Cross, we commend our spirits together with Him into Thy hands. Forsake us not, Father, and remember Your Son's death, through His Resurrection, life has been brought forth, a new soul reborn into Thy Kingdom of Heaven, and bless this unleavened bread through the graces of the Holy Spirit, in the Name of the Father, the Son and the Holy Spirit. Amen."

APRIL 15, 1998

We asked our heavenly mother to place her special blessings on a picture we bought of Jesus after being beaten at the pillar and after the Crowning of Thorns. It isn't a picture, it is Him living before us. Each day that we look at it during prayer, it teaches us that through suffering, you will have eternal salvation into the Kingdom of Heaven. Our heavenly mother said:

"My beloved daughter and son, as you look at that picture, ask yourself, how can *any* human being endure so much suffering and pain? And as you look down on the Cross, ask yourself, how can any human being endure so much pain?

As I stood at the foot of the Cross and looked up, I saw his pain, and I weeped in anguish, and as I stand here before you, my beloved daughter and son, I see pain as you look at that picture and look at the Cross. The pain that my Son endured as your pain, can only be sustained because of love, and it is the love that you both have for our Heavenly Father that allows you to sustain the pain that you do, and the pain that my Son endured at the pillar, and on the Cross, for the love for His people.

Remember, my beloved daughter and son, these words for which I have spoken, and lift up your pains and suffering for the love that you have for your Lord and Savior, Jesus Christ and Our Heavenly Father, for it is this love that will allow you to endure the pains and give you the strength to go forward and carry your crosses. And, as my Son hung on the Cross, he said to His Father, "Father, I love you so, I lift up my soul unto Thee." And so, too, you my daughter and son, must trust our Lord and Savior, Jesus Christ, that He will strengthen your soul and lead you on your journey in doing the work of Our Heavenly Father."

Our heavenly mother asked us to hold the picture up towards her.

PRAYER FROM OUR HEAVENLY MOTHER

"O, Heavenly Father, through love Your Son endured at the beating at the pillar; He shed His Blood for the sins of this world and for the love of mankind. And as the King of Heaven, He wore His Crown of Thorns with pride and humility. And with His hands held tied, He walked in sadness, for He was rejected by His people. But He was never rejected by You, our Father in Heaven. And on the third day, He came into his glory, as the King of Kings, and the Lord of Lords; the Almighty One, the Holy One, to Whom every knee shall bend. For He truly is the King, an everlasting King for eternity, Whose Love, and Mercy, and forgiveness has no end nor beginning. My Son suffered for us all. He became the Sign for the Love, for all His people. And bless this picture that my daughter holds, in the Name of the Father, the Son and the Holy Spirit. Amen."

APRIL 15, 1998

*We purchased Rosary Rings during the Lenten Season. We
asked our heavenly mother to place her blessing upon them.*

*Our heavenly mother asked us to place the rings on each of
our fingers, then to place our hands on top of each others'
hand, so the rings touch. She wanted the cross of each ring
to touch. Then she said:*

"Through my Son, our Lord and Savior,
Jesus Christ, may these rings be the bond
that holds my daughter and son together
through these End Times and into eternity.
May my beloved Spouse grace them with the
peace, joy and happiness when they are
together and may their pains subside in each
other's presence and may their love
increase, and may this love become greater
and greater through the Sacred Heart of My
Son, Jesus Christ and the Immaculate Heart
of me, your heavenly mother. Amen."

MAY 12, 1998

During prayer with our heavenly mother, she gave us a prayer to rebuke Satan during our attacks by him. Our heavenly mother said:

"When you get frustrated, rebuke him in the Name of God. The Holy Water which you carry, you shall spread in the Name of God, and you shall say this prayer:

O, Father in Heaven, protect me from Satan as he attacks me at this hour, and give me the strength to endure the crosses I must bear. I lift up my sufferings for the sins of this world. And in the Name of Jesus Christ, Thy only begotten Son, I rebuke you Satan to the pits of Hell. Amen."

MAY 12, 1998

During prayer with our heavenly mother, at the end of the evening, she said:

"Before I ascend, my chosen children, I shall pray over you, and I shall see you the next-dawn day. We shall discuss the book, we shall discuss the computer, we shall discuss your journey. The beautiful journey that you are on, is a part of a rainbow and as you walk each step, the color, the vibrant colors, of a rainbow in which you walk on are given to you by the sun, and through the sun does the light radiate from the Father. And as this light is delivered to you through the Holy Spirit, you are enveloped in a triangle of the Three In One. Your soul is no longer yours but Our Father's in Heaven, you have given it to Him, and He holds it in His hands, and you will do His work in His Way, and His time, for His time has come."

She then prayed over us:

O, Heavenly Father, as I look up to Heaven I ask for Your intercession through the Holy Spirit. Let my beloved Spouse now descend upon my chosen children and let my Son's Love fill their hearts and souls, and let His Blood fill them, to give them the strength to carry their crosses, as He carried His Cross for the sins of the world. And through the Holy Spirit give them the strength to defend against my Adversary and to rebuke him in the name of You, our Father in Heaven. And through You, O, Father, let the love that exists between them become stronger,

and stronger, and their bond that will lead them to a happy, peaceful, and joyful life. I ask now Father that You bless them, in the name of the Father, the Son and the Holy Spirit. Amen."

She then said:

"Go now in peace and in the love of your heavenly mother, remain strong, my little children, and as you hold each other's hands, hold them tight, support and love each other with the heightened, true love that has been given to you. I bless you with my motherly blessings. I love you my children, I love you my children, I will always love you my children."

JUNE 2, 1998

During prayer with our heavenly mother, after we recited the most holy Rosary, she said to us:

"Continue to love my Son as you have, and always remember what I have foretold you through these End Times: obedience, faith and trust, three virtues. And now, before I leave you, I ask you to both hold out your right hand, and you my son place your right hand on top of her right hand.

She then placed her hands on top of our hands and she said:

"Repeat these words my dearest daughter and son:

O, Father, Our Creator, bless these children. Place Your graces upon them, for these rings that I have blessed and placed upon their fingers will continue to bind them, strengthen them, and they shall remain the most holy objects for which they pray. A covenant that they have with You, for through You O, Father in Heaven, through which all things are made possible, I ask You to bless them through me, through my beloved Spouse, the Holy Spirit, and my Son, our Lord and Savior, Jesus Christ. In the Name of the Father, the Son and the Holy Spirit. Amen."

JUNE 13, 1998

O, heavenly mother, we have met a special friend. His name is Deacon Gerald Geraci, from Our Lady of Mercy Church in Plainville, Connecticut. We have become very fond of him, O, heavenly mother. He has cancer of the eyes. He lifts this cross up to our Heavenly Father each day, a cross which we feel has some fear to it, and we know fear is not of God.

O, heavenly mother, we have a medal we want to give to him. Can you please, O, heavenly mother, give him a prayer that we can give to him from you to help him cope with this eye disease that he has, to let God live within him and him live within God?

As Joseph and I hold forth his medal, O, heavenly mother, we ask you from our hearts and souls to give him a prayer and a blessing of this medal so we can give it to him from you, our heavenly mother.

Our heavenly mother said:

"My dearest daughter, I ask you to hold forth the medal in your hand. Repeat these words for which I speak:

O, Father in Heaven, through Thy graces and the power invested in me I ask you to bless this medal that my chosen children hold forth to Thee. Place Thy graces of healing upon this medal, and let Thy Holy Spirit descend upon this medal, and through the blood that was shed at Calvary by your Son, our Lord and Savior, Jesus Christ, may this medal heal and give strength to those whom it touches.

I ask you, my daughter, to give him this prayer from me:

O, Father in Heaven, as I graciously open my heart and soul unto Thee, and through 'Thy Will be done,' through our Lord and Savior, Jesus Christ, give me the strength to continue to do the work, give me the graces to withstand the temptations of the Evil One, and let my strength continue to lead me on the path of holiness, for I do all for the honor and glory of You, O, Heavenly Father. Thank you for allowing me to serve You and Your Son, Our Lord and Savior Jesus Christ, with all my love, with all my soul, and with all my strength. Amen."

JUNE 13, 1998

Josyp Terelya painted a beautiful picture of Joseph, myself, and one each of our Guardian Angels, Rachel and John. We ask Our heavenly mother to please place a prayer and blessing over our picture. Our heavenly mother said:

"My dearest daughter, place the picture in front of me. Kneel down my dearest daughter, lift up your hands to me:

O, Father in Heaven, I ask You to bless these chosen children in this picture, which represents their faith and trust in You, our Father in Heaven. Continue to guide them in the Light of the Holy Spirit and let the wisdom and knowledge of You, O, Father in Heaven, be given to them so that they will come to understand the Word of God.

I pour forth my motherly blessings through my Immaculate Heart and through my beloved Spouse, the Holy Spirit. I call upon Him to descend upon your hearts and soul at this moment and to fill them with the Love of God the Father.

O, Father in Heaven, I ask for this special blessing in the name of Your Son, our Lord and Savior, Jesus Christ, and through the intercession of St. Theresa, the beloved flower child, and St. Michael the Archangel, and the Guardian Angels John, Rachel, Anthony and Elizabeth. I ask you to pour forth Your blessings in the Name of the

Father, the Son and the Holy Spirit. And may these blessings remain with them throughout time, into the Era of Peace and into Eternity. And may the Choir of angels in Heaven descend upon this room and bless this painting through You, our Father in Heaven. Amen."

The above photo shows Josyp Terelya with Denise and Joseph. The image they are holding is an original painting by Mr. Terelya of Denise and Joseph, and one each of their guardian angels. Denise and Joseph each have two guardian angels given to them by our Heavenly Father. The picture illustrates John, one of Joseph's guardian angels, standing next to Denise; and Rachel, one of Denise's guardian angels, kneeling to the left of Joseph.

JUNE 13, 1998

O, heavenly mother, my sister, Deborah, purchased a beautiful necklace of you holding your Son. Could you, O, heavenly mother, place your special blessings on this necklace for her? She wears this necklace each day and it has been blessed by one of your beloved priests. Our heavenly mother said:

"Hold forth the medal, my daughter, as I place my motherly graces upon it through our Father in Heaven.

O, Father in Heaven, through the power of the Holy Spirit, the Third Person in the Holy Trinity, send forth Your blessings upon this medal through me, Your heavenly mother, and let my motherly love pour forth from this medal to my child. And through the Blood of Your Son, our Lord and Savior, Jesus Christ, let it wash this medal so that the soul becomes strengthened to serve, to understand. And as roses bring sweetness, let Your blessings bring sweetness and strength to her, and through the power invested in me through You, O, Father in Heaven, I bless this medal in the Name of the Father, the Son and the Holy Spirit. Amen."

JUNE 30, 1998

During prayer, we asked our heavenly mother to please bless my sister Deborah's Infant of Prague that she bought.

"O, Father in Heaven, bless this Infant which lies before me, the bearer of all virtues and fruits, the light of the world, the bread of life. And as the seed has been planted, let it sprout and let its growth be strengthened by the prayers of its peoples, and the faithful. And let the Holy Spirit give this child the discernment, understanding and enlightenment of God our Father in Heaven, so that through the baptism of John the Baptist was light brought forth from Heaven into our Lord and Savior, Jesus Christ, for the gift of life is a gift and should be cherished and not taken for granted, and each day in our daily lives we thank our Father in Heaven for this gift and what has been given to us and carry the crosses and bear the pains in union with our Lord and Savior Jesus Christ on the Cross, for we do all for the honor, all for the glory, and all for the being for our Father in Heaven. Amen"

JULY 5, 1998

PRAYER AND BLESSING TO JOSEPH ON HIS BIRTHDAY

Heavenly Mother:

"And now my dearest daughter we will pray together for the gift of the birth of my son, lift up your hands to Our Father in Heaven and repeat these words which I pour forth to thee:

O, Father in Heaven, I thank Thee for this gift of life, I cherish each day as a gift given to me from you. And, as I walk along the journey in life, I grow older and mature so that I may come to understand the gift of life, and through the Holy Spirit, may I be given the knowledge to discern what is right from wrong. And help me each and every day to do right and to rebuke what is wrong, and to remain as a symbol of faith to my Son our Lord and Savior, Jesus Christ, for through Him, life was given to all of us for eternity. And as the sun gives the light to a new dawn day, so has my Son given light to this world and our Father in Heaven has given light in life to the universe. And through our Father in Heaven in union with His Son our Lord and Savior, Jesus Christ, and the Holy Spirit, one body as one in union with each other, may They bless you and give you the strength, love and peace to do the will of thy Father in Heaven. In the name of the Father, the Son and the Holy Spirit. Amen"

JULY 13, 1998

O, heavenly mother, we have a statue of St. Theresa, and we have a statue of Padre Pio, that was given to me as a gift for my birthday, and we have a gift that was given to Denise, by my sister MaryAnn, can you please say a blessing over these for us.

"My dearest daughter and son, please hold the statues up towards me and I shall pray over them with my Motherly Blessings.

O, Father in Heaven, bless this statue of Padre Pio, who served Your Son, with all his heart and strength, and in his hands he held the marks of Your Son's crucifixion on the cross. And through the stigmatas on his hands he healed spiritually and physically those who came before him. And as a servant of you O, Father in Heaven, I ask You to allow the Holy Spirit to descend upon this statue and bless it, in the name of the Father, the Son and the Holy Spirit. And may this blessing rest upon this statue and may Padre Pio remain with my chosen children as a protector and as a guide on their journey. Amen.

My beloved St. Theresa, the fragrance of your roses still continue to be poured forth to my Son our Lord and Savior, Jesus Christ. You embrace his cross with your heart and soul and still today remain within

your heart and soul. You gave your life to my Son, you lived your life according to my Son, and now you live in union with my Son, as a Saint and intercessor for all of my children. Continue to shower my children with your roses, continue to act as the intercessor to them as receiving their prayers and bringing them to my Son our Lord and Savior, Jesus Christ, continue to pray with my children the most Holy Rosary, and within your hands you hold your salvation, teach my children the salvation of my Son, the salvation of their souls and lead them on the road to holiness, to the Kingdom of my Son, our Lord and Savior, Jesus Christ. And Father, bless this statue in the name of the Father, the Son and the Holy Spirit. Amen.

And now I ask you, my daughter, to hold up the picture of the church that lies before you. O, Father in Heaven, through me your heavenly mother, bless this church that my child holds in her hands, bless it with Your love that this church will stand the test of time, and through its persecutions Your church shall stand forever, for the love of God is for eternity. And as the church was built on a rock, so too is the faith of my daughter and son, and it too shall withstand the test of time, and within the heart and soul will the church exist, and each day they shall receive their strength from my Son our Lord and Savior, Jesus Christ. Bless this gift in my daughters hand through the power of the Holy Spirit, in the name of the Father, the Son and the Holy Spirit. Amen."

AUGUST 13, 1998

"O, heavenly mother, I would like Father George to hold up his prayer beads, and for you O, heavenly mother to pour forth your motherly graces upon them. Could you please do that for him?" Our heavenly mother said:

"Pray with me my dearest little children:

O, Father in Heaven, pour forth Thy Graces, and let thy Holy Spirit descend upon these children in giving them the enlightenment, discernment and understanding of Thy Word.

For within my hands I hold the weapon against Satan. In these the Most Holy Rosary I pray with all my heart and soul in serving You, Our Father in Heaven, and may You bless me in the Name of the Father, the Son and the Holy Spirit. And I pour forth my Motherly Love to the most Holy Rosary for my Beloved Priest. Amen."

"O, heavenly mother, we are doing a talk at My Father's Retreat House this weekend in Moodus, Connecticut. Please allow the Holy Spirit to enter into us and let us touch the lives of many of Our Father's children. Could you please give us a prayer for us to say when we do our talks, this prayer can be either said out loud to your children or for Joseph and I to say before we begin?"

"My dearest daughter and son, continue to recite the Holy Spirit prayer that I have given you.

Per your request, my dearest little daughter, recite this prayer in your hearts only:

O, Father in Heaven as I stand before Your children, let Thy words flow from my heart and soul through my lips and rest upon their hearts and souls. And as the seed bears its fruits let Your Divine Words bear the fruits of love. And let Your words guide them and show them the way to the path of holiness. Bring Wisdom and Knowledge to me through the Holy Spirit and through Thy name let the Blood that Your Son shed at Calvary cover me and protect me from the snares of the Enemy and from those who try to harm me as I speak Your words. And let Thy light from Heaven come down upon me and surround me and give me the glow of love and divine graces. And let this light shine forth and illuminate the eyes of those that stand before me and let them see that in me You live and flourish forever. Amen."

SEPTEMBER 3, 1998

Denise said, "O, Heavenly Mother, we purchased Our Lady of Grace statues for Joseph Hunt and Dr. Joseph Vitolo. When should we give them these statues, and would you like to say a prayer for these statues?"

"My dearest little daughter did I not ask you to get these statues for my children?"

Denise replied: "Yes, you did."

"And you have remained obedient to me, your heavenly mother? It is up to you to decide when you wish to give these statues to them. I will place my blessing upon them. Place the statues in your hands and repeat the words after me. No my dearest little daughter, kneel before me."

Our heavenly mother continued:

"O, Father in Heaven, Whose joys are eternal and goodness imperishable, teach my children the affections towards Heaven. And through the graces of the Holy Spirit, infused with the Sacred Heart of our Lord and Savior Jesus Christ and the Immaculate Heart of Your heavenly Mother, bless these statues O, Father in Heaven, in the name of the Father, Son and Holy Spirit. And protect my children. Guide them and strengthen them with the blood mixed with water and through Thy Holy Fear, so that they may be one in union with Thy Holy Family and seers of eternal Life. Amen"

Our heavenly mother then said: "Remain here, my dearest daughter. Open up your arms. I now place my motherly hands upon your forehead.

O, Father in Heaven, before me lies my beloved daughter. Continue to give her the strength to endure the pains and sufferings of the crosses that she carries upon her shoulders. Her faith and trust in me, her heavenly mother, sustains her each day. I present her to You, O, Heavenly Father. Her obedience is a sign of her trust in You, her Creator. Let my beloved Spouse, the Holy Spirit, descend upon her and fill her heart and soul with His presence.

Remember, my dearest little daughter, I am your heavenly mother. I love you very much. I watch over you each and every day. Continue to remain strong for me. And soon, you shall see everything as which I foretold you given to you in thy Father's Name.

Go now in my peace, in my motherly love. Your tears are not of sadness, but of joy, for very few of my children have what you have. Your faith sustains you. And as my Son has spoken to you, you are my little sheep that reigns in His Sacred Heart. And you shall bear the fruits from all that you have been given, for many of my children will now come to you.

You will now open up your heart and soul and pour forth the love that has been given to you, to them.

I love you, my dearest little daughter. Remain strong for me, your heavenly mother. I am always with you and I shall never abandon you. And as I have said, I never promised you that there would be no pain, no suffering. But always remember what our Lord and Savior, Jesus Christ, did for us all. And never once did He complain; never once did He show fear; never once did He show doubt; never once did He show confusion. And what He did, I wish you to do. And remember these words: '**Father I trust in You and love You. I commend my spirit into Thy hands.**'

Go now, my daughter. Go now in my peace and keep this in your heart and soul. And there you shall feel my warmth and love embrace you always."

SEPTEMBER 13, 1998

During prayer with our heavenly mother, she requested that we burn the petitions that are given to us after three days of lifting them up during prayer. We are then to collect the ashes and we are to bury them in a Rose Garden, and we are to consecrate the rose garden to her. Below is a prayer that she gave us to consecrate the rose garden to her. We asked her how we do this and she said to us:

"My dearest daughter and son, you will use the consecration prayer that I have given to you, that which I ask to be consecrated each day. Use the name, Oh Rose Garden To Thy Mother We Give Thee. And after you consecrate say these words:

Father in Heaven, these roses I give to thee to be presented to our heavenly mother. Send down Your angels to watch over them, protect them from the evil one. For these roses will be given to your peoples to heal them, to guide them, to strengthen them.

These gifts that you have given us we bless with this holy water in the name of the Father, the Son and the Holy Spirit. Amen."

"O, heavenly mother, we have two things upon which we would like you to place your graces and your prayers. The first thing O, heavenly mother, is the basket that lies before you from your children at your cenacle. They have placed their religious articles and pictures into this basket for your graces. O, heavenly mother, through the Will of Our Father in Heaven and through you, please place your special blessings upon each object in this basket.

We told your children that we would type out the prayer and blessing for each of them as a special gift for them from you and from us your 'Two Hearts as One.'" She said:

"My dearest daughter and son, pray with me, pray with me over these religious articles that lie before thee. Hold up your hands to heaven and repeat the words after me:

O, Father in Heaven, I call upon thee, allow my Beloved Spouse the Holy Spirit to descend upon these holy articles that lie before me. O, Father in Heaven, through the blood and water which gushed forth from the side of your Son, let it wash and cleanse these religious articles and fill them with thy holy presence. And let the light kindled with love, allow your holy name to become enflamed for eternity, and let thy graces rest upon them with your Son our Lord and Savior, Jesus Christ. In the name

of the Father, the Son and the Holy Spirit. Amen."

"The second article O, heavenly mother, is for my twin sister Deborah and it lies before me. It is a beautiful Cross of your Son and our Lord and Savior, Jesus Christ. Please O, heavenly mother, through thy Will of Our Heavenly Father, place your special graces upon this Cross." She said:

"My dearest daughter, hold the Cross up towards me. Tell your sister that her Heavenly Mother asks her to do this:

I sent her my motherly love. She is to take this crucifix and place it above where she lies. Each morning when she rises, she is to place her hands on my Son's feet and she is to say these words:

O, Lord Jesus Christ, my Savior and Shepherd I trust in thee for my protection and guidance this day. Please watch over me and give me the strength to do thy will be done. I love you Lord, for what you have given to me. Protect and watch over me this day, I give this day to you. I love you with all my heart and soul, and bless me in the name of the Father the Son and the Holy Spirit. Amen.

And now I ask Our Father in Heaven to place His graces and blessings upon this cross in the name of His Son our Lord and Savior, Jesus Christ.

Father, before me lies your Son who died for Your peoples' sins. And as he stood on the Cross and looked up to You, Father and

said, 'I commend my Spirit into thy hands, I love thee Father, forsake me not for what I ask.' I ask, Father, that you Bless Your Son on this Cross in the Name of the Father, the Son and the Holy Spirit. Amen."

KEY TO THE TRIUMPH
The Final Marian Dogma

A Film By **The MaxKol Institute**

A documentary highlighting the theological, historical, and mystical foundations of the Final Marian Dogma

Mary Coredemptrix, Mediatrix, and Advocate

This film offers an explanation of these titles from some of the leading theologians and clergy in the word, and features:

- The words of Pope John Paul II about Coredemptrix, Mediatrix, and Advocate
- How the messages of Rue du Bac, Fatima, Akita, and LaSalette are all connected to this Dogma
- Why this Dogma is the key to unlock the door to inestimable graces for the world, and why it will bring THE TRIUMPH of the Immaculate Heart
- The prophecy of Don Bosco about the end of the 20th century
- The prophecies of Ida Peerdeman of Amsterdam
- Why the Dogma is the key to peace in the world
- Learn why it is endorsed by 42 Cardinals, 500 bishops, and 5 million faithful

$15.95 plus shipping & handling, 58 minutes

The Thunder of Justice
by Ted & Maureen Flynn

Order Form

"This book has changed my life."

That's been the response of readers of **The Thunder of Justice.** Nearly all are profoundly changed by reading the words of warning and hope given today by Our Lady. Now you can bring these same powerful words to your friends and loved ones. Share Heaven's urgent warnings and ultimate promise of victory—by sending them their own copy of **The Thunder of Justice.** Use the convenient order form below!

Now let it change your friends.

Order today! Send your mail orders to **MaxKol Communications, 1301 Moran Road * Suite 303 * Sterling, VA 20166.** Phone orders: 703-421-1300. Fax orders: 703-421-1133

❏ Yes, I want to order a copy of Thunder of Justice for $15.95 plus $4.50 shipping and handling. I have included an additional $15.95 plus shipping and handling per book to cover the cost of sending more than one to the same address. (Spanish available—$13.95 plus $4.50 S&H)

My Name _____

Address _____

City, State, Zip _____

Phone (h)_____(o) _____

Recipient of book (if different from sender above)

My Name _____

Address _____

City, State, Zip _____

Phone (h)_____(o) _____

MASTERCARD/VISA/CHECK